(Engage! Press is a division of EdSuccess)

The Parent Playbooks

2nd Edition
Fun and Enjoyable Learning Activities with Kids

GRADES 3 - 5

Standards-Based Learning Activities

- Parent-Teacher tested
- Parent-Teacher contributed
- Fun ways to learn new ideas and apply old ones

Dr. Joni Samples

The Parent Playbooks: Grades 3 - 5

© 2019 ENGAGE! Press
Printed and bound in the United States of America

All rights reserved. Written permission must be secured from the publisher and author to use or reproduce any part of this book except for brief quotations in critical reviews or articles. To order additional copies, please contact the Publisher, Engage! Press at:

ENGAGE! Press
2485 Notre Dame 370-170
Chico, CA 95928
www.engagepress.com
ENGAGE! Press is a division of EdSuccess

This book contains information gathered from many sources. The printer, publisher, and author disclaim any personal liability, either directly or indirectly, for advice or information presented within. Although the author, publisher, and printer have used care and diligence in the presentation, and made every effort to ensure the accuracy and completeness of the information contained in this book, we assume no responsibility for errors, inaccuracies, omissions, or any inconsistency herein.

First Printing 2019
ISBN No. 978–0–9906335-3-2
Library of Congress Cataloging–in–Publication Data

DEDICATION

The Parent Playbook series is dedicated to the memory of Linda Armstrong. Linda was a lover of books and literature, a librarian and writer, my editor and keeper of databases, believer in families and learning, and, above all, my friend.

ABOUT YOUR PARENT PLAYBOOK

Dear Parents,

Welcome to the Parent Playbook series, where you will find recipes for learning. Similar to a cookbook, each activity begins with a list of needed materials, the time required to complete the activity, and a description of the activity. Instead of a "daily nutritional requirement," these recipes relate to State Educational Standards for learning. The activities are easy and fun.

I am a lifelong educator with four children. During my child rearing days, my cooking rarely came from a cookbook. Meal planning consisted of whatever I could recall from my childhood or what would heat up quickly in the microwave.

My interest in assisting my children in education focused on, like my menu for meals, something quick, easy, and able to make a positive difference in a fun way. However, there was nothing available on the market that gave me easy directions and ideas to help my children become successful learners. I dredged stuff up from my teaching days or depended on their schools to provide something. But, homework didn't entertain me or my children enough to do more than what was due the next day. We would lose interest, so I began creating other activities to do.

It was then that my husband suggested that I write a column in the newspaper to share the activities with other parents. As the newly elected County Superintendent of Schools in our area and someone who wanted to let folks know I was on the job, that sounded like a winning idea. I could provide teachers, parents, and myself with home activities that were easy, fun and enhanced learning.

One day a colleague remarked, "That muffin activity sure did a lot of measuring of fractions. Which grade level standard is that?" Of course! Share activities and match them to the learning standards taught in the classroom and everyone wins. With that the idea for the Parent Playbooks was born.

Parents enjoy a fun learning time with their children. The activities they do together reinforce concepts taught at school. The teachers see the support from home reflected in the children's schoolwork. In addition, the kids — their grades, test scores and self-confidence are off the charts. So, here you have recipes for learning in the form of Parent Playbooks.

Taste, benefit from, and most of all experience the delicious joy of learning with your children.

Sincerely,
Dr. Joni

A Letter from Dr. Joni and Trinidad:

To the Kids

Trinidad says hi and welcome to The Parent Playbooks — a place where learning is fun!

You might think Trinidad learns mostly at the beach, but this is one starfish that gets around town. Grocery stores, movies, pizza parlors, and the library are just a few of the spots Trinidad is likely to show up. See how often you can find Trinidad as you play and learn through the activities shared with you in this book. Don't forget to create your own activities. There is plenty of room for you and your family to write in the "What We Learned Today" section. Let Trinidad "Star" in new ways to learn and play.

Enjoy the activities along with Trinidad and Make Learning Fun!

Sincerely,

Dr. Joni and Trinidad

Table of Contents

About the Learning Standards		1
English Language Arts		3
	Grade 3	6
	Grade 4	24
	Grade 5	38
	Blank - Ready for more activities	52
Math		55
	Grade 3	58
	Grade 4	66
	Grade 5	73
	Blank - Ready for more activities	78
Science		81
	Grade 3	84
	Grade 4	90
	Grade 5	99
	Blank - Ready for more activities	102
Science		105
	Grade 3	116
	Grade 4	121
	Grade 5	126
	Blank - Ready for more activities	132

INDEX	134
ACTIVITIES FORM	138
ORDER FORM	141

For workshops or presentations by Dr. Joni, contact Family Friendly Schools:

Phone or Fax: 1-530-899-8423
www.familyfriendlyschools.com

ABOUT THE LEARNING STANDARDS

The standards used in the Parent Playbook series are a combination of Common Core and State Standards for English Language Arts and Math.

The standards used in this material are a representation of all state learning standards and are tested in every state.

The major purpose for use of the standards is to provide teachers and parents a guideline for skills taught at each grade level.

Standards for Science and Social Studies are tested in every state. Science and Social Studies activities for parents are included here and matched to a set of standards derived from standards from across the United States.

We do hope these activities will be both enjoyable and filled with learning for both parents, teachers, and, most importantly, your children.

ENGLISH LANGUAGE ARTS

3 – 5

Parent Playbook Activities

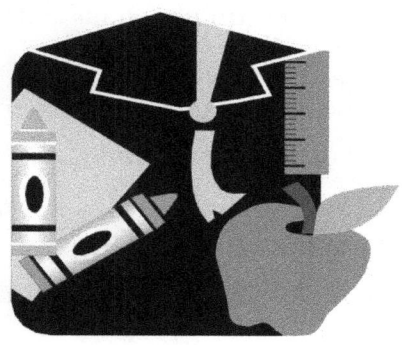

Want to add your favorite activity to the next Parent Playbook?
Use the convenient form in the back of this book or contact the publisher at:

www.familyfriendlyschools.com • www.engagepress.com

By Dr. Joni SamplesEnglish Learning Arts Standards

ENGLISH LANGUAGE ARTS LEARNING STANDARDS
Grades 3-5

The purpose for English Language Arts (ELA) Standards is to guarantee that all students develop the language skills they need to succeed in life as informed, productive members of society.

The ability to read and write begins before children enter school as they experience and experiment with language activities – from babbling to learning sounds and words.

Children begin to make connections between reading, writing, speaking, and listening as a way of gathering information and learning about the world around them.

The ELA Standards are listed on the following page to help you understand and put together all the skills needed to read and write. No standard stands alone. They all work together to create a language arts program.

Basic Topics of the Core English Language Arts Learning Standards - Grades 3-5

Reading Standards for Literature
    Key Ideas and Details
    Craft and Structure
    Integration of Knowledge and Ideas
    Range of Reading and Level of Text Complexity

Reading Standards for Informational Text
    Key Ideas and Details
    Craft and Structure
    Integration of Knowledge and Ideas
    Range of Reading and Level of Text Complexity

Reading Standards Foundational Skills
    Phonics and Word Recognition
    Fluency

Writing Standard
    Text Types and Purposes
    Production and Distribution of Writing
    Research to Build and Present Knowledge
    Range of Writing

Speaking and Listening Standard
    Comprehension and Collaboration
    Presentation and Knowledge of Ideas

Language Standard
    Conventions of Standard English
    Knowledge of Language
    Vocabulary Acquisition and Use

Books for Kids

Number of People: 2 Time: 30 minutes Grade Level **3**

Materials: Book Club order form

Description: During a television commercial, look over the Arrow, Lucky, or Troll Book Club selections your child brings home from school. Let your child choose three books he would like to read. The books from these companies are inexpensive, fun and, geared to their interest and reading level. When the books arrive, turn off his least favorite TV show and read one of the books or a chapter together. Do this every night until the books are all read. Be sure to ask questions about each book. What happened in the story? What was your child's favorite part? What other ending could there have been? Which book was the favorite?

ENGLISH LANGUAGE ARTS STANDARD

Reading Standards for Literature: Key Ideas and Details

1. Ask and answer questions to demonstrate understanding of a text, referring explicitly to the text as the basis for the answers.

Comics Aloud

Number of People: 2 Time: 15 minutes Grade Level **3**

Materials: Newspaper with comics

Description: While you read the newspaper, have your child look at and read the comics. Ask her what happened in the comic strip and why it was funny. What did the pictures tell her? My brother learned to read by reading comic books at night at the kitchen table.

ENGLISH LANGUAGE ARTS STANDARD

Reading Standards for Literature: Key Ideas and Details

2. Recount stories, including fables, folktales, and myths from diverse cultures; determine the central message, lesson, or moral and explain how it is conveyed through key details in the text.

What day of the week do you go to the library?

Library Days

Number of People: 2   Time: 30 minutes   Grade Level: 3

Materials: Library

Description: There are fewer activities as satisfying as a day at the library. When my children were young, Tuesday was library day. We went to the library after school to check out books, do research or just study. Tuesday was our special day. We probably paid enough overdue book fines to have a wing of the library dedicated to our family, but at least I knew they were readers. They are still readers in their adulthood. Take your kids to the library and get yourself a book or two while you're at it. It will be relaxing for you and they will have fun too. What books are your "stars" favorites?

ENGLISH LANGUAGE ARTS STANDARD

Reading Standards for Literature: Craft and Structure

6. Distinguish their own point of view from that of the narrator or those of the characters.

What we learned today...

_____

_____

_____

_____

_____

_____

Books and More Books

Number of People: Family Members   Time: An hour   Grade Level **3**

Materials: Books

Description: My family used every opportunity to get new books for us to read at home. However, buying books from a bookstore every week can be expensive. There are other, less expensive ways to enjoy a new book: weekly trips to the library, yard sales, and library book sales. School book clubs, like Arrow and Lucky, keep you out of the poorhouse and provide readable material that you can buy at a fraction of the cost. You can even organize a book exchange with families in the neighborhood. Another idea is to ask relatives to give books or bookstore gift certificates for birthdays and Christmas along with a toy. My children always had a wonderful time after Christmas going to the bookstore with Grandma's gift certificates.

ENGLISH LANGUAGE ARTS STANDARD

Reading Standards for Literature: Range and Level of Text Complexity

10. By the end of the year, read and comprehend informational texts, including history/social studies, science, and technical texts, at the high end of the grades 2-3 text complexity band independently and proficiently.

What we learned today...

_____

_____

_____

_____

_____

_____

Read the Board

Number of People: 2 or more   Time: 10 - 20 minutes

Grade Level **3**

Materials: Informational Books—Social Studies, Science

Description: Remember flannel boards? Some of us do. To make a flannel board all you need is a piece of board, cardboard, or tag-board approximately 3 feet by 2.5 feet. Cover it in flannel of any color. Have your child read an informational book, draw or cut out pictures from a magazine to explain the book, glue flannel to the back of the picture, and use the flannel board and pictures to tell you about the book. From baseball heroes to sport cars to rock stars, this is a hit.

ENGLISH LANGUAGE ARTS STANDARD

Reading Standards for Informational Text: Key Ideas and Details

1. Ask and answer questions to demonstrate understanding of a text, referring explicitly to the text as the basis for the answers.

Bake a Cake

Number of People: 2   Time: 30 minutes

Grade Level **3**

Materials: Recipe, ingredients for your recipe

Description: Have your child read a recipe to you while you bake a cake, make cookies, or prepare any other kitchen delight. He can measure the water, oil, and other ingredients while you stir. Make sure he reads the recipe aloud several times so you get it just right. This is also a good time to discuss fractions and the value of math.

ENGLISH LANGUAGE ARTS STANDARD

Reading Standards for Informational Text: Craft and Structure

4. Determine the meaning of general academic and domain-specific words and phrases in a text relevant to a grade 3 topic or subject area.

Read the Kitchen

Number of People: 2   Time: 15 minutes   Grade Level **3**

Materials: Reading materials around the room
Description: Have your child "read the kitchen."
What notes are stuck on the refrigerator?
What is on the back of the cereal box?
What ingredients are in a can of soup?

Ask questions about what she is reading. Have a conversation about what is in a can of soup. The discussion will make the reading have meaning for her.

ENGLISH LANGUAGE ARTS STANDARD

Reading Standards for Informational Text: Craft and Structure
7. Use information gained from illustrations and the words in a text to demonstrate understanding of the text.

Favorite Stories

Number of People: 2   Time: 30 minutes   Grade Level **3**

Materials: Reading materials
Description: Your child has favorite stories and by now favorite authors. He may have a series he really likes—*Goosebumps* or *Harry Potter*. Set aside fifteen minutes during dinner to have a regular chat about his favorites. Talk about the stories and the characters. Why is it a favorite? What is different about this story from other stories he knows and what is the same? How do the characters change or stay the same?

ENGLISH LANGUAGE ARTS STANDARD

Reading Standards for Literature: Integration of Knowledge and Ideas
9. Compare and contrast the themes, settings, and plots of stories written by the same author about the same or similar characters.

Famous Read

Number of People: 2 Time: 10 minutes Grade Level **3**

Materials: Informational Books—Social Studies, Science

Description: Third grade is the first year children begin to read about subjects for information; social studies (history) and science. Reading for information is a different skill than reading a story with a beginning, middle and end. So, have your child try it out now and it will be easy when the reading gets more complex.

A good place to start training for more difficult reading is to read books about famous people; historical personalities, ballplayers, actors. Who is your child's favorite famous person? Encourage him to learn all the facts (social studies) possible about his famous person. The person's life will come alive and your child's information reading skills will advance.

ENGLISH LANGUAGE ARTS STANDARD

Reading Standards for Informational Text: Range of Reading and Level of Complexity
10. By the end of the year, read and comprehend informational texts, including history/social studies, science, and technical texts, at the high end of the grades 2-3 text complexity band independently and proficiently.

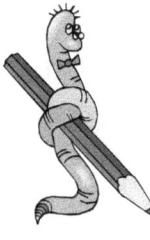

What we learned today...

_____

_____

_____

_____

_____

Hang Man

Number of People: 2   Time: 10 minutes

Grade Level **3**

Materials: Paper and pencil

Description: Hangman is a game that has been around for decades and has been a favorite of children for just as long. It is quite possible your child has played this game at one time or another. Now you can use it too. It will help with spelling, vocabulary and critical thinking. You can fit in a game of Hangman almost anywhere. It only takes a few minutes. Kids will love to stump you with their words and, in the process, have you hang the poor man. If you haven't played before, here's how:

1. On a piece of paper draw a hangman's scaffold complete with noose.
2. Have your child think of a word but keep it a secret. Below the scaffold, your child puts blank lines corresponding to the number of letters in the word he has chosen.
3. You begin by guessing letters one at a time. If your letter is in the word, he puts the letter on the blank where it goes. If the letter is not in the word, he draws a part of the body (a head, arm, leg, eye, etc. Guess the word before the man is hanged and you win.

ENGLISH LANGUAGE ARTS STANDARD

Reading Standards: Foundational Skills: Phonics and Word Recognitions
3. Know and apply grade-level phonics and word analysis skills in decoding words.

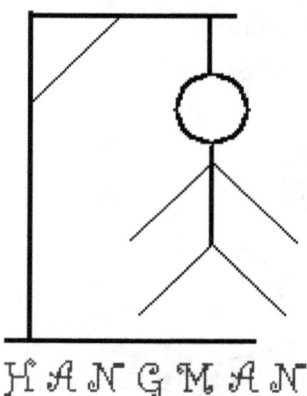

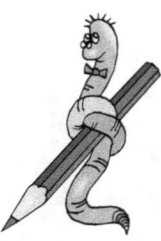

What we learned today..

_____

_____

_____

_____

_____

_____

Weekly Recipe

Number of People: 2   Time: 15 minutes   Grade Level **3**

Materials: Your favorite recipe book

Description: Kids love to eat and by now they have their favorite foods. To help with both eating and reading, let your child choose a favorite recipe for the week. Maybe it's chocolate chip cookies or spaghetti. You choose a time to make the delectable, and he will read you the recipe as you cook. It would help with math too if he measures the ½ cups of sugar and the ¼ cup of butter. Ask him to read the recipe several times so you can get it just right.

ENGLISH LANGUAGE ARTS STANDARD

Reading Standards: Foundational Skills: Fluency
4. Read with sufficient accuracy and fluency to support comprehension.

Kid Magazines

Number of People: 2   Time: 30 minutes or so   Grade Level **3**

Materials: Magazine subscriptions

Description: Magazines written specifically for children are fun and provide short and interesting stories for your child to read silently or aloud. Publications like *Ranger Rick*, *Scholastic*, or *Boy's/Girl's Life*, and *Highlights* are inexpensive magazines you can order over the Internet. These publications are easy enough for most early readers. You, the adult can hear how easily words are read and understood when your child reads to you aloud. Besides, you get to hear a story and maybe learn something new as well.

ENGLISH LANGUAGE ARTS STANDARD

Reading Standards: Foundational Skills: Fluency
4. Read with sufficient accuracy and fluency to support comprehension.

Movie Review

Number of People: 2   Time: 30+ minutes   Grade Level 3

Materials: Movie, Paper and Pencil

Description: Most kids love movies; however, when the show is over they leave the theater and that's the end of the learning. Next time go one step further. Have your child write a movie review after he watches a movie. He can be a movie critic. Did he like the show? What did he like best? Who would enjoy watching it? Did he like the ending? How would he change the ending to make it better?

ENGLISH LANGUAGE ARTS STANDARD

Writing Standards: Text Types and Purposes

1. Write opinion pieces on topics or texts, supporting a point of view with reasons.

Notes

Number of People: 2   Time: 20 minutes   Grade Level 3

Materials: Paper and pencil

Description: Leaving for work early? Leave a note for your child. Reading a note makes for good reading practice as well as practice in following directions.

If he is just starting to learn cursive, leave your note in cursive writing so he can get used to seeing it. Have him respond to you in a note written in cursive as well.

ENGLISH LANGUAGE ARTS STANDARD

Writing Standards: Text Types and Purposes

2. Write informative/explanatory texts to examine a topic and convey ideas and information clearly.

Vacation Diary

Number of People: Family   Time: 1 - 2 weeks   Grade Level **3**

Materials: Diary

Description: Vacation time is a great time to introduce writing skills to your child. She can log in such details as: Where did she have breakfast? What time did she get to the restaurant? At which restaurant did she eat? Was it good? How much did it cost? Where did she travel for the day? What was the best part of the day?

Many things happen on a vacation. Have her write about each part of the day.

ENGLISH LANGUAGE ARTS STANDARD

Writing Standard: Text Types and Purposes

2. Write informative/explanatory texts to examine a topic and convey ideas and information clearly.

What we learned today...

___
___
___
___
___
___

Cartoon Balloons

Number of People: 2 Time: 30 minutes

Grade Level **3**

Materials: Paper, colored pencils or crayons, pencil

Description: Draw a couple of cartoon characters, including *Trinidad the Starfish*. Even stick-figures are great. Put bubbles above their heads and let your child fill in the bubbles with a dialogue of his choice.

I'm a "Star!" How about you?

ENGLISH LANGUAGE ARTS STANDARD

Writing Standards: Text Types and Purposes

(3b) Use dialogue and description of actions, thought, and feelings to develop experience and events or show the response of characters to situations.

What we learned today...

_____

_____

_____

_____

_____

_____

Directions

Number of People: 2   Time: 30 minutes   Grade Level **3**

Materials: Paper and pencil

Description: Have your child give you directions. A fun way to do this one is to ask your child to tell you in writing how to make a peanut butter sandwich. Tell her you are going to follow her directions exactly. As she reads her directions to you, follow her words exactly. If she tells you to put peanut butter on the bread, you may have to do it with your fingers if she fails to tell you to use a knife. She will figure out quickly how important it is to give ALL the steps. Do this activity with different tasks such as telling you how to fix the salad for dinner or change the DVD. Your child will improve her level of detail each time.

ENGLISH LANGUAGE ARTS STANDARD

Writing Standards: Production an Distributions of Writing

4. With guidance and support from adults, produce writing in which the development and organization are appropriate to task and purpose.

Pen Me

Number of People: 2   Time: 10 minutes   Grade Level **3**

Materials: Pencil and paper

Description: Third grade is the time where a child moves from printing to cursive writing. Practice those new skills whenever possible. Have her write in a journal. Have her write notes to you about where she wants to go or what she wants to do this week. Have her write out the grocery list.

Gently work with spelling and punctuation too. Remember this is a lot to learn, and she needs lots of praise for her progress.

ENGLISH LANGUAGE ARTS STANDARD

Writing Standards: Production and Distribution of Writing

5. With guidance and support from peers and adults, develop and strengthen writing as needed by planning, revising, and editing.

Writing More Email Letters
Number of People: 2   Time: 30 minutes or so

Grade Level **3**

Materials: Computer with Internet access

Description: While you are emailing friends, let your child email too. Send emails to grandparents or cousins—someone who will write back—and bring up return emails for them to read and answer. Be sure to have him edit his emails before sending. This is great writing and reading reinforcement.

ENGLISH LANGUAGE ARTS STANDARD

Writing Standard: Production and Distribution of Writing

6. With guidance and support from adults, use technology to produce and publish writing as well as to interact and collaborate with others.

Wishes and Dreams
Number of People: 2   Time: 15 minutes

Grade Level **3**

Materials: Magazines, scissors, paste, construction paper

Description: We all have dreams about what we want to have, do, or be. Let your child create a "dream board" around something he would like to have or do. Use magazines from which he can cut out pictures of his interests and dreams, and then paste them on tag-board to put in his room. Perhaps he would like to have a bicycle or a pair of special shoes. Ask him to find the pictures, articles, and other information so he can become the expert on the things he wants and why he wants them. Now that he has done the research, it is time to talk about how he plans to achieve his dream.

ENGLISH LANGUAGE ARTS STANDARD

Writing Standards: Research to Build and Present Knowledge

7. Conduct short research projects that build knowledge about a topic.

Hi Kids - I like Dora the Explorer, especially when she's finding "stars."

TV Talk

Number of People: 2   Time: 30 minutes

Grade Level **3**

Materials: TV

Description: You know you will be watching TV programs with your child. From *Sesame Street* when he is a preschooler to *CNN* when he's an adult. Get in the habit of talking about the shows you watch together. What does he think about the topic(s) of the show? What is his opinion? What does he think the show is suggesting? Are the ideas good ones for him?

ENGLISH LANGUAGE ARTS STANDARD

Speaking and Listening Standards: Comprehension and Collaboration

1. Engage effectively in a range of collaborative discussions with diverse partners of grade 3 topics and texts, building on others' ideas and expressing their own clearly.

What we learned today...

_____

_____

_____

_____

_____

_____

_____

Project Practice

Number of People: 2   Time: 15 minutes

Grade Level **3**

Materials: Pictures, objects, charts if appropriate
Description: Kids often have projects and activities to do at school. Sometimes they are required to give an oral presentation including main ideas and supporting information. Have your child practice his presentation for you. Let him tell you about his project. Ask questions. Help him be clear about what it is that he is trying to tell you.

ENGLISH LANGUAGE ARTS STANDARD

Speaking and Listening: Comprehension and Collaboration
2. Determine the main ideas and supporting details of a text read aloud or information presented in diverse media and formats, including visually, quantitatively, and orally.

What we learned today...

_____

_____

_____

_____

_____

_____

Play It

Number of People: 2   Time: 15 minutes   Grade Level **3**

Materials: None

Description: Have your child choose a favorite story. Let her act out the story she has chosen. See if you can guess the name of the story. You may need a few hints, but try to guess it from clues the acting provides. The better she gets at acting, the easier it will be to guess.

ENGLISH LANGUAGE ARTS STANDARD

Speaking and Listening Standards: Presentation of knowledge and Ideas

5. Create engaging audio recordings of stories or poems that demonstrate fluid reading at an understandable pace; add visual displays when appropriate to emphasize or enhance certain facts or details.

Ordering Out

Number of People: 2+   Time: 10 minutes   Grade Level **3**

Materials: Telephone

Description: Have your child call for the pizza tonight.

Dialing a phone number, speaking clearly, asking for what he wants, and answering questions, are all skills that take practice. Besides, the family gets a pizza if he does it right!

ENGLISH LANGUAGE ARTS STANDARD

Speaking and Listening Standards: Presentation of Knowledge and Ideas

6. Speak in complete sentences when appropriate to task and situation in order to provide requested detail or clarification.

Topical Questions
Number of People: 2   Time: 15 minutes   Grade Level 3

Materials: None

Description: When things get a little dull in the car on a trip to the store, ask your child to pick a topic. Give her one minute to think about her topic, then one minute to tell what she can about that topic. For example, she may choose chickens as her topic. Give her one minute to tell everything she knows about chickens. Then you have a minute to ask questions about her topic while she gives you answers. Be sure to have her speak in complete sentences when she is relating the facts she knows and when she answers the questions. If you ask what color a chicken is, she must say, "Chickens come in all colors". A partial answer to the question like, "lots of colors" does not count. This is a great time for recalling facts, creating sentences, and sharpening thinking skills.

ENGLISH LANGUAGE ARTS STANDARD

Speaking and Listening Standards: Presentation of Knowledge and Ideas

6. Speak in complete sentences when appropriate to task and situation in order to provide requested detail or clarification.

Crosswords
Number of People: 2   Time: 30+ minutes   Grade Level 3

Materials: Children's crossword puzzle books

Description: When you read the paper, show your child the daily crossword. It will be too hard for him and maybe too hard for you! Magazines like *Highlights* have crossword puzzles he can do. Let him do a crossword at his level of ability while you finish the paper or tackle the crossword yourself. Bet he does better than you!

ENGLISH LANGUAGE ARTS STANDARD

Language Standards: Conventions of Standard English

1. Demonstrate command of the conventions of standard English grammar and usage when writing or speaking.

What are some favorite words of your TV "stars?"

New Words from TV
Number of People: 2 or more   Time: 10 - 20 minutes

Grade Level **3**

Materials: TV

Description: Kids watch TV so let's make watching TV into something that will help build the number of words they know. During a favorite show, jot down a few words that might be new or used in a different way than usual. Talk about what the words mean during the commercials. If no one is quite sure, look the word up in the dictionary.

ENGLISH LANGUAGE ARTS STANDARD

Language Standard: Vocabulary Acquisition and Use

4. Determine word meanings (based on grade 3 reading).

What we learned today...

___
___
___
___
___
___

Who "stars" in your favorite story?

What is the Theme?
Number of People: 2   Time: 30 minutes

Grade Level **4**

Materials: Book

Description: As your child is reading a new book or story, ask him to tell you the theme of the piece. What point is the author trying to make? What is the story about? What does he suppose will happen next? Looking beyond the happenings in the story and thinking about what the author wants him to learn, strengthens skills of critical thinking and remembering details.

ENGLISH LANGUAGE ARTS STANDARD

Reading Standards for Literature: Key Ideas and Details

2. Determine a theme of a story, drama, or poem from details in the text; summarize the text.

What we learned today...

_____

_____

_____

_____

_____

_____

It's a Myth
Number of People: 2   Time: 10 - 20 minutes

Grade Level **4**

Materials: Books or Internet with mythology stories
Description: On your next trip to the library or bookstore, get a book at a fourth grade level on myths. Ask the librarian. She will help. There are many mythological figures of old, Hercules, Apollo, Zeus, to name only a few. Their stories are fanciful, intriguing, and adventurous.

Read the stories together while your child figures out his favorites. What words are there in myths that are not in other stories? Which ones do you like best?

ENGLISH LANGUAGE ARTS STANDARD

Reading Standards for Literature: Craft and Structure
4. Determine the meaning of words and phrases as they are used in a text, including those that allude to significant characteristics found in mythology.

Books and Movies
Number of People: 2   Time: 30 minutes

Grade Level **4**

Materials: Book Club book order form
Description: This time when you look over the Arrow, Lucky, or Troll Book Club selections your child brings home from school, let your child choose a favorite book that is also a movie or TV show. Read the book together when it arrives. Then watch the movie or TV show. Discuss with your child several questions. What was the same? What was different? Which did he like best and why. What is the next book/movie you want to try?

ENGLISH LANGUAGE ARTS STANDARD

Reading Standards for Literature: Integration of Knowledge and Ideas
7. Make connections between the text of a story or drama and a visual or oral presentation of the text, identifying where each version reflects specific descriptions and directions in the text.

Library Days Too

Number of People: 2   Time: 30 minutes   Grade Level **4**

Materials: Library

Description: If you have started visiting the library, keep going. If you haven't, start now. It's a very inexpensive way to get different books in the house every week. Stories are great reading practice and adding a play or a poem now and then spices up the reading as well. Your child can even act out the play for you or read the poem to a little brother, sister, or pet. Sometimes pets stay and listen longer than a sibling does.

ENGLISH LANGUAGE ARTS STANDARD

Reading Standards for Literature: Range of Reading and Level of Complexity
10. By the end of the year, read and comprehend literature, including stories, dramas, and poetry, in the grades 4-5 text complexity band proficiently, with scaffolding as needed at the high end of the range.

Magazines

Number of People: 2   Time: 30 minutes   Grade Level **4**

Materials: Magazine subscriptions

Description: Do you have any magazine subscriptions? Get one more for your child. *Ranger Rick* or *Sports Illustrated for Kids* are good ones. Let him read his magazine while you read yours. Share your favorite articles. Have your child tell you about his favorite people, sports, or events. Let him explain his favorite player's averages or most recent feats.

ENGLISH LANGUAGE ARTS STANDARD

Reading Informational Text: Key Ideas and Details
1. Refer to details and examples in a text when explaining what the text says explicitly and when drawing inferences from the text.

Hi Kids - my favorite magazines are about movie "stars."

Reading Around You
Number of People: 2   Time: 15 minutes

Grade Level **4**

Materials: Reading materials around the room

Description: Have your child read his bedroom. What notes are stuck on the wall/bulletin board? What books are in the bookcase? What does it say on his trophy? What note did grandma just send him for his birthday? When he is stuck on a word, let him try to figure it out.

ENGLISH LANGUAGE ARTS STANDARD

Reading Standards: Foundational Skills: Phonics and Word Recognition

3. Know and apply grade-level phonics and word analysis skills in decoding words.

What we learned today...

_____

_____

_____

_____

_____

_____

Page 27

Listen to the Reading

Number of People: 2   Time: 30 minutes

Grade Level **4**

Materials: Reading materials

Description: Listen to your child read to you as you work around the house. You can determine at what level he is reading and what books will be best for him to read. As he reads, notice how hard the material is that he is reading. Pick a section of about 100 words and let him read it. You check the errors made. 0-4 errors: the material is easy and he can read it to you or by himself. 5-10 errors: the material is appropriate for you to read together. 10 or more errors: The material is too hard and you should read this one to him.

ENGLISH LANGUAGE ARTS STANDARD

Reading Standards: Foundation Skills: Fluency

4. Read with sufficient accuracy and fluency to support comprehension.

What we learned today...

_____

_____

_____

_____

_____

_____

TV Review

Number of People: 2   Time: 30+ minutes

Grade Level **4**

Materials: TV, paper and pencil

Description: TV watching is usually included in some part of the day's activities. Make the time more useful by asking your child to write a review of the show she has just watched. If it was especially good, make sure she lets you know how good it was. You may want to watch the show or you may want to let her watch it again—that will probably depend on the review she has written.

ENGLISH LANGUAGE ARTS STANDARD

Writing Standard: Text Types and Purposes

1. Write opinion pieces of topics or texts, supporting a point of view with reasons and information.

You Have Mail

Number of People: 2   Time: 15 minutes

Grade Level **4**

Materials: Magazines, pencil, post cards or paper and pencil, envelop and stamp

Description: Kids like to get and read mail. Let them go through a magazine for things they would like to order. They will need to send a letter or postcard (writing practice), wait for a return (patience), and read what comes in the mail (reading practice). It is exciting for a child to go to the mailbox and find a letter addressed in her name.

ENGLISH LANGUAGE ARTS STANDARD

Writing Standards: Production and Distribution of Writing

4. Produce clear and coherent writing in which the development and organization are appropriate to task, purpose, and audience.

Family Newspaper
Number of People: Family Time: 30 minutes Grade Level 4

Materials: Computer, program to do newspaper writing

Description: Create your own family newspaper. Everyone in the family can write a story about something they are doing. Having a newspaper or newsletter publishing program on your computer makes writing easier. Once written, have each family member read his or her story aloud. As your child hears her story, let her edit it so that it becomes even clearer. Then after everything is completed, it is time to print it out and distribute to friends and families. One of my children liked to edit and another liked to add pictures. All in all, we loved the excitement of seeing our names in print.

ENGLISH LANGUAGE ARTS STANDARD

Writing Standards: Production and Distribution of Writing

5. With guidance and support from peers and adults, develop and strengthen writing as needed by planning, revising, and editing.

Reports
Number of People: 2 Time: 45 minutes Grade Level 4

Materials: Paper and pencil

Description: Kids start writing reports around grade four. To give him a head start in school, ask him to write a report on the new toy he wants. He will have to research it, find the prices, the color he wants, where it can be purchased, and figure out how he is going to pay for it!

ENGLISH LANGUAGE ARTS STANDARD

Writing Standards: Research to Build and Present Knowledge

7. Conduct short research projects that build knowledge through investigation of different aspects of a topic.

Hi Kids - I like to "Star" in my own journal. How about you?

Daily Journal
Number of People: 2+   Time: 10 minutes   Grade Level **4**

Materials: Journal

Description: Journal writing is a good way to remember a day's events. At the end of the day, have your child spend 10 minutes jotting down the events of the day. You can use a special notebook for this activity. Every once in a while, ask him to read one of his favorite events. That will let him know you are interested and you can help him make sure his journal accounts make sense.

ENGLISH LANGUAGE ARTS STANDARD

Writing Standards: Range of Writing

10. Write routinely over extended time frames and shorter time frames for a range of discipline-specific tasks, purposes, and audiences.

What we learned today...

_____

_____

_____

_____

_____

_____

Hi Kids - One of my favorite recipes is cuSTARd.

Ordering In
Number of People: 2   Time: 30 minutes

Grade Level **4**

Materials: Recipe books and rest of the family

Description: At our house, we let the kids make dinner once in a while. They loved discussing what they would fix, and what everyone's favorite dishes were. My son, Christopher's favorite dish month after month was stew. So let your kids review recipes, discuss and decide.

You may want to monitor preparation a bit just to be on the safe side.

ENGLISH LANGUAGE ARTS STANDARD

Speaking and Listening: Comprehension and Collaboration

1. Engage effectively in a range of collaborative discussions (one-on-one, in groups, and teacher-led) with diverse partners on grade 4 topics and texts, building on others' ideas and expressing their own clearly.

What we learned today...

_____

_____

_____

_____

_____

_____

Your Video is Showing
Number of People: 2   Time: 30+ minutes

Grade Level **4**

Materials: None

Description: Watching a favorite video is fun. The nice thing about videos or DVDs is you can stop them part way through and talk about what's happening. Do just that and ask your child to tell you what's going on. What's going to happen next? How do you think the show will end? He can even record a short version of his own video on a cell phone or video camera paraphrasing and acting out the story he viewed.

ENGLISH LANGUAGE ARTS STANDARD

Speaking and Listening Standards: Comprehension and Collaboration
2. Paraphrase portions of a text read aloud or Information presented in diverse media and formats, including visually, quantitatively, and orally.

Anecdotes are Personal Accounts
Number of People: 2   Time: 15 minutes

Grade Level **4**

Materials: Special objects

Description: Information reads better when it comes with stories and anecdotes. Give your child an object he's familiar with, like a favorite baseball glove, a skateboard, or a seashell. Let him think of the reason why it is a favorite. Have him tell you a story or real life happening about why it is important to him. Maybe the baseball glove was signed by his favorite player or he won it. The skateboard may have belonged to a friend and the seashell picked up while on a great vacation. Let him tell you about his object. Encourage lots of details.

ENGLISH LANGUAGE ARTS STANDARD

Speaking and Listening Standards: Comprehension and Collaboration
3. Identify the reasons and evidence a speaker provides to support particular points.

Weekly Readers Plus
Number of People: 2   Time: 15 minutes

Grade Level **4**

Materials: *Weekly Reader* or *Scholastic Magazine*

Description: Your child has probably been bringing home *Weekly Reader* or *Scholastic Magazine*. Reading those magazines with him helps with understanding. Now let him read an article and report on what he is reading. Ask questions if you are not clear about what he is telling you. If you don't have a *Weekly Reader*, just pick out a readable magazine article or a favorite story from one of your magazines.

ENGLISH LANGUAGE ARTS STANDARD

Speaking and Listening Standards: Comprehension and Collaboration

4. Report on a topic or text, tell a story, or recount an experience in an organized manner, using appropriate facts and relevant, descriptive details to support main ideas or themes; speak clearly at an understandable pace.

Write-to-Me Grammar
Number of People: 2   Time: 20 minutes

Grade Level **4**

Materials: Paper and pencil

Description: Coherent and legible writing takes practice. Make sure your child has plenty of practice. Write notes to him and expect him to write notes back to you. You don't need a red pen to correct what he writes, but help him use words correctly. You can also point out the nouns, verbs, adjectives, and other grammar facts. Try something like: "Good Morning. I hope you are having an awesome day. There is a treat in the refrigerator for you. Let me know how you like it."

Grammar facts: Noun; a person, place or thing.

Adjective: a word used to describe something. For example, "He has red hair." "Red" is the adjective.

Verb: an action word—words like, hit, jump, laugh, run, etc.

ENGLISH LANGUAGE ARTS STANDARD

Language Standards: Conventions of Standard English

1. Demonstrate command of the conventions of standard English grammar and usage when writing or speaking.

Write-to-Me Spelling

Number of People: 2 Time: 20 minutes

Grade Level **4**

Materials: Paper and pencil

Description: Writing notes in school may get your child in trouble, but it doesn't have to at home. Have your child write notes to you. When he wants to go to the ball game, have him write you a note about requesting it and telling why he wants to go. When he wants a special dinner, ask him to write you a note. When he wants to tell you what he wants for his birthday, tell him to write you a note. A note will help you know exactly what he wants, where to find it, and how much it costs. If the words in his note aren't spelled correctly, tell him it is important to get it right because you might misunderstand and get the wrong thing!

ENGLISH LANGUAGE ARTS STANDARD

Language Standards: Conventions of Standard English
2. Demonstrate command of the conventions of standard English capitalization, punctuation, and spelling when writing.

What we learned today...

_____

_____

_____

_____

_____

Once you STARt talking, it's hard to stop!

Talk Time	Grade Level **4**
Number of People: 2 Time: 30 minutes	

Materials: None

Description: One of the easiest things you can do to help build your child build vocabulary is to talk. Talk in the car, while doing dishes, or sorting laundry. Talk about what you are doing, where you are going, where the dishes come from, how something is made, or anything else your discussion warrants. Clarify new words. As your child reads those new words, he will already have talked about what those words mean so they won't be hard to understand.

ENGLISH LANGUAGE ARTS STANDARD

Language Standard: Vocabulary Acquisition and Use

4. Determine or clarify the meaning on unknown and multiple-meaning words and phrases based on grade 4 reading and content, choosing flexibly from a range of strategies.

What we learned today...

_____

_____

_____

_____

_____

_____

Read Everything Again

Number of People: 2+ Time: 10 - 20 minutes Grade Level 4

Materials: Items in the room with words and messages

Description: You've done this before, but we're going to do more of it. Let your child read anything around you; cereal boxes, labels, recipes, phone books, signs, billboards, shopping lists, menus, TV Guides, or comics in the newspaper. This time, have him pick out the words that have some sort of action or emotion like, whirred, spent, cried. Ask: What is the topic that created the action or emotion?

ENGLISH LANGUAGE ARTS STANDARD

Language Standard: Vocabulary Acquisition and Use

6. Acquire and use accurately grade-appropriate general academic and domain-specific words and phrases, including those that signal precise actions, emotions, or states of being and that are basic to a particular topic.

Quotes

Number of People: 2   Time: 30 minutes or so

Grade Level **5**

Materials: Book

Description: As your child is reading a new book, ask him to quote his favorite parts to you. Then you can talk about what those quotes mean both to you and to him. A quote is a word for word repeating or copying of the words someone has said or written.

ENGLISH LANGUAGE ARTS STANDARD

Reading Standards for Literature: Key Ideas and Details

1. Quote accurately from a text when explaining what the text says explicitly and when drawing inferences from the text.

Library Days with a New Twist

Number of People: 2   Time: 30 minutes

Grade Level **5**

Materials: Library

Description: On days you and your child go to the library, she will probably go for the books she already knows and likes. Guide her to choose books that have topics about things she is studying in school. What is she studying in her Social Studies class? There are many new things to learn about the subjects that she is learning in school. Just one book in a different area opens up all kinds of new adventures and contributes to making her more knowledgeable about the subject.

Example: If her class is learning about Native American tribes, choose a book that talks about Native American beauty tips or games the children played.

ENGLISH LANGUAGE ARTS STANDARD

Reading Standards for Informational Text: Key Ideas and Details

3. Explain the relationships or interactions between two or more individuals, events, ideas, or concepts in a historical, scientific, or technical text based on specific information in the text.

STARt your reading engine today!

Chapter Books
Number of People: 2   Time: 15 minutes

Grade Level **5**

Materials: Books with chapters in them

Description: Early reading books have short stories in them. In the middle reading grades children are reading books that have chapters that build one on the other, leading to a great ending. Have your child choose chapter books like *Treasure Island* or a book from the *Harry Potter* series. Have him tell you which chapter he is on, what has happened so far, and what is happening in the chapter he is currently reading.

ENGLISH LANGUAGE ARTS STANDARD

Reading Standards for Literature: Craft and Structure

5. Explain how a series of chapter, scenes, or stanzas fits together to provide the overall structure of a particular story, drama, or poem.

What we learned today...

_____

_____

_____

_____

_____

_____

I wonder if my ancestors were dinosaurs? Maybe dino"stars"?

Movie Time

Number of People: 2   Time: 15 minutes   Grade Level **5**

Materials: TV

Description: Choose a show or a movie to watch when your child has already read the book. *Harry Potter* or *Jurassic Park* is possible here, but there are plenty more. Ask how the show adds to the meaning or tone of the book. How does the show make the story different and how are they similar?

ENGLISH LANGUAGE ARTS STANDARD

Reading Standards for Literature: Integration of Knowledge and Ideas

7. Analyze how visual and multimedia elements contribute to the meaning, tone, or beauty of a text (e.g., graphic novel, multimedia presentation of fiction, folktale, myth, poem).

What we learned today...

_____
_____
_____
_____
_____
_____
_____

What Was That?

Number of People: 2   Time: News time

Grade Level **5**

Materials: News shows on TV

Description: Have your child read information from a book about a favorite topic. Then read a second piece of information about the same topic. Another book or the Internet will have information. What new ideas did you find in the second piece? What was in the first one that was not in the second? What differences are there in the two? Now read a third and see what new things you find this time.

ENGLISH LANGUAGE ARTS STANDARD

Reading Standards for Informational Text: Craft and Structure

5. Compare and contrast the overall structure of events, ideas, concepts or information in two or more texts.

Vacation Research

Number of People: 2+   Time: Several days or so

Grade Level **5**

Materials: Computer with word processing program

Description: We had our kids research the Internet for where they wanted to go on our summer vacations. They researched different locations, gathered information about those locations, then chose a location and wrote a report about why we should visit there. They needed to explain the benefits, clearly define the reasons for their choices, and research the costs in order to stay within our budget. They needed to use complete sentences and correct spelling. We chose one of their vacation spots and had a great time.

ENGLISH LANGUAGE ARTS STANDARD

Reading Standards for Informational Text: Integration of Knowledge and Ideas

7. Draw on information from multiple print or digital sources, demonstrating the ability to locate answers to a question quickly or to solve a problem efficiently.

It's in the News
Number of People: 2   Time: 15 minutes   Grade Level 5

Materials: Internet homepage news
Description: There are all kinds of news updates on the Internet these days. Choose a news report and read all the information you can find about it. Then, take time to talk about what you learned making sure to include the facts.

Example: If the Florida coast experiences a hurricane, learn the facts about what happened. Which towns did the hurricane hit hardest? Who did the rescuing? What kind of warnings did the weather departments issue?

ENGLISH LANGUAGE ARTS STANDARD

Reading Standards for Informational Text: Integration of Knowledge and Ideas
9. Integrate information from several texts on the same topic in order to write or speak about the subject knowledgeably.

Scrabble
Number of People: 2 or more   Time: 60+ minutes   Grade Level 5

Materials: Scrabble game
Description: Scrabble is a great game for spelling and language development. We played it often and we didn't just "let" the children win. They had to come up with their own words. Triple letter scores with a Q or a Z were bonuses.

ENGLISH LANGUAGE ARTS STANDARD

Reading Standards Foundational Skills: Phonics and Word Recognition
3. Know and apply grade-level phonics and word analysis skills in decoding words.

Make yourself a "star" at reading by reading something everyday.

Listen to the Reading
Number of People: 2 Time: 30 minutes

Grade Level **5**

Materials: Reading materials

Description: You've done this before, but now it's a different grade level. Listen to your child read to you. Notice how hard the material is that he's reading. Pick a section of about 100 words and let him read it. You check the errors made. 0-4 errors -- it's easy and he can read it to you or by himself. 5-10 errors -- good for you to read together. 10+ errors -- too hard, but you could read this one to him.

ENGLISH LANGUAGE ARTS STANDARD

Reading Standards Foundational Skills: Fluency

4. Read with sufficient accuracy and fluency to support comprehension.

What we learned today...

___
___
___
___
___
___

Please 'splain STARdom to me.

"Splain It"
Number of People: 2   Time: 15+ minutes   Grade Level 5

Materials: Children's crossword puzzle books

Description: Lucy from the Peanuts cartoons used to explain to Charlie how things worked. She would "splain" it to him. Have your child "'splain" in writing what he wants to do for the weekend. If it's a ball game he wants to go to, have him "splain" how it's played or why he wants to go or how you figure out who wins. If your daughter wants to bake cookies, have her "splain," in writing, which cookies she'll bake and just why she picked those cookies. A lot of things need "splaining."

ENGLISH LANGUAGE ARTS STANDARD

Writing Standards: Text Types and Purposes

2. Write informative/explanatory tests to examine a topic and convey ideas and information clearly.

What we learned today...

___
___
___
___
___
___

Penmanship Plus

Number of People: 2   Time: 60 minutes

Grade Level 5

Materials: Paper and pencil

Description: Pick a topic of the week and write notes back and forth about it. Make sure he can understand what you are saying and that he makes his ideas clear to you. If you can't read his writing you'll need to return it for a rewrite. If you don't understand his statements, ask him to clarify them—in writing of course!

ENGLISH LANGUAGE ARTS STANDARD

Writing Standard: Production and Distribution of Writing

4. Produce clear and coherent writing in which the development and organization are appropriate to task, purpose, and audience.

Reporter Rewrite

Number of People: Family   Time: 30+ minutes

Grade Level 5

Materials: Small notebook, paper and pencil or computer

Description: Most news reporters keep notes in a little notebook, but when it comes to writing their stories, they write and rewrite. Have your child be a reporter. Let him write a news story about something going on in your family. Help him revise the story until it is just right. Then send it to other families through the United States mail or in an email. Give it a catchy headline and watch the interest it will bring.

ENGLISH LANGUAGE ARTS STANDARD

Writing Standard: Production and Distribution of Writing

5. With guidance and support from peers and adults, develop and strengthen writing as needed by planning, revising, editing, rewriting or trying a new approach.

Electronic Writing

Number of People: 2   Time: Several days

Grade Level **5**

Materials: Computer with word processing program

Description: Most kids start using computers early these days. Often times computers are merely used for games and email, but in the upper grades computers are an excellent tool for making report writing easier. Your child can do the research on the computer, print out pictures and facts, and write the report. When my son had to report on volcanoes, he was able to do the research, decide which facts were most important for the report, and then choose what illustrations were best to explain the topic. There is much to learn on any subject. Using a computer to research and write the material eliminates massive rewrites that can make the project too overbearing.

ENGLISH LANGUAGE ARTS STANDARD

Writing Standard: Research to Build and Present Information

7. Conduct short research projects that use several sources to build knowledge through investigation of different aspects of a topic.

Reports with Support

Number of People: 2   Time: 45+ minutes

Grade Level **5**

Materials: Paper and pencil

Description: Kids can write reports about any topic. They will pick the areas they like and will be able to tell you all kinds of fun facts. Have them write a report about their favorite topic based on information they have read from books, the Internet or other reading materials about the subject. If the topic is about something you can visit, go!

ENGLISH LANGUAGE ARTS STANDARD

Writing Standards: Production and Distribution of Writing

9. Draw evidence from literary or informational texts to support analysis, reflection, and research.

Have you used your "star"tling imagination today?

Writing Your Own Story
Number of People: 2   Time: 30+ minutes

Grade Level **5**

Materials: Book, paper and pencil

Description: Stories are great places to find ideas for writing. After reading a favorite story, let your child write one with the same characters but with a different plot or a different ending to the author's story. If your child is reading weekly, this approach makes a great book report as well as helps with writing skills. Perhaps your child will want to write a novel with its own characters and situations. Creative writing is fun and it is possible to do it over an extended period.

ENGLISH LANGUAGE ARTS STANDARD

Writing Standards: Range of Writing

10. Write routinely over extended time frames and shorter time frames for a range of discipline-specific tasks, proposes, and audiences.

What we learned today...

_____

_____

_____

_____

_____

_____

Don't forget to talk about the "stars" of the movie.

Take 20

Number of People: 2   Time: 30+ minutes   Grade Level 5

Materials: Movies, paper and pencil

Description: Movies are still a favorite for most kids. On the way home after a movie or when you've finished watching a movie on TV, Take 20. Take 20 minutes to talk about the movie. How did you like it? What was so good about it? What special effects were cool? Or whatever goes with this particular show. Enjoy the 20.

ENGLISH LANGUAGE ARTS STANDARD

Speaking and Listening Standards: Comprehension and Collaboration

1. Engage effectively in a range of collaborative discussions (one-on-one, in groups, and teacher-led). With diverse partners of grade 5 topics and texts, building on other ideas and expressing their own clearly.

What we learned today...

_____

_____

_____

_____

_____

PowerPoint
Number of People: 2   Time: 15 minutes

Grade Level 5

Materials: Computer and PowerPoint software program

Description: Putting together a report can get more exciting when you using something visual to display your message. A basic PowerPoint® program includes slides for each part of your child's report where words and graphics can be included to show what she wants to say. You will want to help with this one if it is the first time your child uses the program. It is a little complicated, but it won't be long before you'll be learning from her.

Hint: Print out the slides and place them in the report.

ENGLISH LANGUAGE ARTS STANDARD

Speaking and Listening: Presentation of Knowledge and Ideas

5. Include multimedia components and visual displays in presentations when appropriate to enhance the development of main ideas or themes.

Crostics
Number of People: 2   Time: 30+ minutes

Grade Level 5

Materials: Children's crossword puzzle books with crostics

Description: Crosswords are great new word gatherers. So are crostics. There are word puzzles found in crossword puzzle books that eventually spell out a sentence or phrase. There are also word puzzles with hidden secret clues and messages to discover. Try them tonight and see what happens.

ENGLISH LANGUAGE ARTS STANDARD

Language Standards: Conventions of Standard English

2. Demonstrate command of the conventions of standard English capitalization, punctuation, and spelling when writing.

Talking Down

Number of People: 2   Time: 5 minutes   Grade Level 5

Materials: A younger child

Description: We often hope to have kids use language—words and sentences—at their own grade level, but sometimes making things more understandable for a younger child helps them improve their own use of language. Explaining to a younger child or sibling how to put together a puzzle or play a game allows your child to choose words that are easier to understand. Let him try it. It will make a difference to them both.

ENGLISH LANGUAGE ARTS STANDARD

Language Standards: Knowledge of Language

3. Use knowledge of language and its conventions when writing, speaking, reading or listening.
   a. Expand, combine, and reduce sentences for meaning, reader/listener interest, and style.

Proverbial Sayings

Number of People: 2   Time: 20 minutes   Grade Level 5

Materials: Book with proverbs

Description: Check out a book from the library that contains old sayings, adages, and proverbs. You remember sayings like, "Cat got your tongue," or "A stitch in time saves nine." Kids may not have heard these sayings before and may not know what they mean. Enjoy explaining how the cat does not really have your tongue. It just means that you do not have anything to say. And, for our second sentence, if you fix things now, it will save time later because things won't get worse. Ask the librarian to point out a book on sayings and their meanings.

ENGLISH LANGUAGE ARTS STANDARD

Language Standards: Vocabulary Acquisition and Use

5. Demonstrate understanding of figurative language, word relationships, and nuances in word meanings.
   b. Recognize and explain the meaning of common idioms, adages, and proverbs.

What we learned today...

Create your own playbook activities!

Language Arts

Number of People: Time: Grade Level

Materials:

Description:

ENGLISH LANGUAGE ARTS STANDARD

Language Arts

Number of People: Time: Grade Level

Materials:

Description:

ENGLISH LANGUAGE ARTS STANDARD

Create your own playbook activities!

Language Arts		Grade Level
Number of People:	Time:	

Materials:
Description:

ENGLISH LANGUAGE ARTS STANDARD

Language Arts		Grade Level
Number of People:	Time:	

Materials:
Description:

ENGLISH LANGUAGE ARTS STANDARD

MATH

3 – 5

Parent Playbook Activities

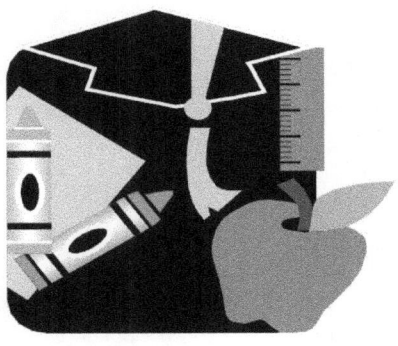

Want to add your favorite activity to the next Parent Playbook? Use the convenient form in the back of this book or contact the publisher at:

www.familyfriendlyschools.com • www.engagepress.com

By Dr. Joni Samples   Math Learning Standards

MATH LEARNING STANDARDS
Grades 3-5

Grade 3:
    Number & Operations in Base Ten
    Number & Operations—Fractions
    Measurement and Data
    Geometry
    Operations & Algebraic Thinking

Grade 4:
    Number & Operations in Base Ten
    Number & Operations—Fractions
    Measurement and Data
    Geometry
    Operations & Algebraic Thinking

Grade 5:
    Operations & Algebraic Thinking
    Number & Operations in Base Ten
    Number & Operations—Fractions
    Measurement & Data
    Geometry

My Stars, I really do enjoy eating. When are we going shopping again?

Grocery Math

Number of People: 2   Time: 45 minutes

Grade Level **3**

Materials: Trip to the grocery store, pencil and pad

Description: Once a week I find myself at the grocery store with one or more of my children. They help. One checks prices and sales. Is the 22 oz. jar for $1.98 a better deal than the 44 oz. jar for $4.05? Another keeps a running tally of how much we've spent so we don't go over budget. I give the other child the coupons. She finds the coupon items and keeps track of what else we need to find. It takes a lot to feed us. They stay busy.

MATH LEARNING STANDARD

Mathematics: Operations & Algebraic Thinking

3. Use multiplication and division within 100 to solve word problems in situations involving equal groups, arrays, and measurement quantities.

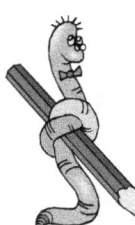

What we learned today...

_____

_____

_____

_____

_____

_____

Breakfast Multiplication

Number of People: 2   Time: 15 minutes   Grade Level 3

Materials: Placemats with math problems on them

Description: Give your child a great morning start in doing math. Placemats with math problems are great fun! How much is 2x3? How about 2x2? Do you know 3x4? After he does the problems, give him an answer. What is the problem that has the answer of 4? Have him point out the problem with the highest answer. You can make up all kinds of variations for this activity. Just keep doing the multiplication. If you can't find the placemats you need, you can just write four or five math examples on regular paper and use them for placemats.

MATH LEARNING STANDARD

Mathematics Operations & Algebraic Thinking

7. Fluently multiply and divide within 100, using strategies such as the relationship between multiplication and division or properties of operations. By the end of Grade 3, know from memory all products of two one-digit numbers.

How Much

Number of People: 2   Time: 15 minutes   Grade Level 3

Materials: Groceries, money

Description: If you estimate your groceries will be $37.00, ask your child what bills he would give the clerk to pay for the groceries. If you give the clerk two $20 bills how much would you get back? If you gave the clerk a fifty-dollar bill, what would your change be? Get creative. Try other combinations.

MATH LEARNING STANDARD

Mathematics: Operations & Algebraic Thinking

8. Solve two-step word problems using the four operations.

Pizza Night

Number of People: 2   Time: 15 minutes

Grade Level **3**

Materials: Menu from your favorite pizza place

Description: When we want pizza at my house, we need more than one. Everyone has his or her own favorite toppings. If pizzas are $16.00 for a cheese pizza and 75 cents per topping, how much is it going to cost for three pizzas, one with pepperoni and sausage, one with olives and mushrooms, and one with onions? Try other combinations and watch the math skills grow.

MATH LEARNING STANDARD

Mathematics: Operations & Algebraic Thinking

8. Solve two-step word problems using the four operations.

Family Math Night

Number of People: Many   Time: 2 hours

Grade Level **3**

Materials: Your school's Family Math Night

Description: Schools often have a Family Math Night. Plan to go. Stations are set up around the cafeteria with math games and activities. When we go, one of my children is adding the score on a bean bag toss while another is building a tower with toothpicks. I am still looking for the best strategy for playing Mancala. Just one more time and I'm sure I'll beat my 9-year-old.

Everyone will have plenty of math to do.

MATH LEARNING STANDARD

Mathematics: Operations & Algebraic Thinking

9. Identify arithmetic patterns, and explain them using properties of operations.

Find the numbers quick before someone reSTARts the car.

License Math

Number of People: 2+   Time: 30 minutes

Grade Level **3**

Materials: A trip in the car

Description: Read the license plate number from the cars around you excluding the letters. For example: KGT 4783 would be four thousand seven hundred and eighty three. Ask him to round the number up to the nearest 10, 100, or 1000.

MATH LEARNING STANDARD

Mathematics Number & Operations in Base Ten

1. Use place value understanding to round whole numbers to the nearest 10 or 100.

What we learned today...

_____

_____

_____

_____

_____

_____

STARt your engine on this one!

License Numbers

Number of People: 2 or more   Time: 30 minutes

Grade Level **3**

Materials: A trip in the car, license plates

Description: While traveling, have everyone choose a license plate from a vehicle around them. Write the numbers on a sheet of paper and see who can add them the fastest.

MATH LEARNING STANDARD

Mathematics Standards: Number & Operations in Base Ten

2. Fluently add and subtract within 1000 using strategies and algorithms based on place value, proprieties of operations, and/or the relationship between addition and subtraction.

What we learned today...

___

___

___

___

___

___

Kitchen Measuring

Number of People: 2   Time: 30 minutes

Grade Level **3**

Materials: Recipe, measuring cups, bowls

Description: Your child can practice measuring while you bake a cake. Let him use your 1/4 measuring cup to see how many times it takes to fill a 2-cup bowl with water. Add the 1/4 cups together. Then try it with spoons, 1/2 cups, and different size bowls. You may need to mop the kitchen when you are done, but he will have learned a great deal about fractions.

MATH LEARNING STANDARD

Mathematics: Number and Operations—Fractions

3. Explain equivalence of fractions in special spaces, and compare fractions by reasoning about their size.

Time to Tell

Number of People: 2+   Time: 10-20 minutes

Grade Level **3**

Materials: Clock

Description: Digital clocks have made telling time a bit easier, so your child may not have seen a clock face. Take time to show them the 12 hours on the clock. Have him figure out what time he gets up, eats breakfast, goes to school, gets home, has dinner, goes to bed, or any other normal activity. Be sure he tells you in hours and minutes when all of these events occur. Every once in a while, ask him what time it is. Of course, you can look at the clock, but it is more fun if he tells you.

MATH LEARNING STANDARD

Mathematics: Measurement & Data

1. Tell and write time to the nearest minute and measure time intervals in minutes, Solve word problems involving addition and subtraction of time intervals in minutes.

How Much for the Week?
Number of People: 2   Time: 30 minutes   Grade Level **3**

Materials: None

Description: We have four teenagers. How many 1/2 gallons of milk do they drink during the week? Let someone keep track at your house. How many quarts is that? How many cups? If one of them is gone for a week, how much less milk would you buy? How much would that be in grams?

MATH LEARNING STANDARD

Mathematics: Measurement & Data

2. Measure and estimate liquid volumes and masses of objects using standard units of grams. Add subtract, multiply, or divide to solve one-step word problems involving masses or volumes that are given in the same units.

We Need How Much?
Number of People: 2   Time: 30 minutes   Grade Level **3**

Materials: Tape Measure, ruler, pencil, and paper

Description: Are you putting in a new carpet, building a bookcase, or adding a fence? Let your child help measure what you need. You will probably want to check for accuracy, but make sure you get to the half and quarter inch range. You want to be sure you get it just right.

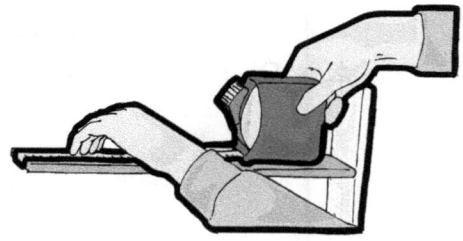

MATH LEARNING STANDARD

Mathematics: Measurement & Data

4. Generate measurement data by measuring lengths using rulers marked with halves and fourths of an inch.

Could you guess that my favorites are "star" shaped?

Cookie Shapes
Number of People: 2   Time: 1 hour

Grade Level **3**

Materials: Cookie mixture

Description: Usually we make round cookies, but this time make them differently. Make them in geometric shapes. How about making triangles, squares, and rectangles? Now change the shape and make that rectangle into a rhombus. All of the four-sided shapes are quadrilaterals. Octagons have eight sides. Pentagons have five sides. What else can you make? Hint: Sugar cookies are easier to cut into shapes than most other kinds.

MATH LEARNING STANDARD

Mathematics: Geometry

1. Understand that shapes in different categories (e.g., rhombuses, rectangles and others) may share attributes (e.g., having four sides), and that the shared attributes can define a larger category (e.g., quadrilaterals). Recognize rhombuses, rectangles, and squares as examples of quadrilaterals that do not belong to any of these subcategories.

What we learned today...

_____

_____

_____

_____

_____

_____

I especially like the Texaco stations with the "star" on them!

Mileage

Number of People: 2 Time: 15 minutes Grade Level **4**

Materials: Car at the gas station

Description: We all have to stop for gas for our cars regularly. While you are waiting for the tank to fill, ask your child if a gallon of gas costs $3.47, how much will it cost if you get 10 gallons? How much will 15 gallons cost? How many more questions can you ask?

MATH LEARNING STANDARD

Mathematics: Operations and Algebraic Thinking
2. Multiply or divide to solve word problems involving multiplicative comparison.

What we learned today...

_____
_____
_____
_____
_____

Worth the Time
Number of People: 2+   Time: A week at a time   Grade Level 4

Materials: Weekly allowance

Description: Add another $5 to your child's weekly allowance. Charge him a quarter for every half-hour he watches TV. Whatever he has left over at the end of the week, he keeps. It will be interesting to see what he values most, his television or his allowance. The math part comes in when figuring out how much money he has left out of the $5.

MATH LEARNING STANDARD

Mathematics: Operations and Algebraic Thinking

3. Solve multistep word problems posed with whole numbers and having whole-number answers using the four operations, including problems in which remainders must be interpreted.

Catalog Days
Number of People: 2   Time: 45 minutes   Grade Level 4

Materials: A catalog

Description: Give your child a budgeted amount of money and a catalog. Have your child go through the catalog and choose items he likes. Give him a budget and let him add up his choices to see if he can stay under his limit. He may have to change his choices to stay within budget. Remind him it is pretend or he must at least wait until his birthday.

MATH LEARNING STANDARD

Mathematics: Operations & Algebraic Thinking

3. Solve multistep word problems posed with whole numbers and having whole-number answers using the four operations, including problems in which remainders must be interpreted.

Time Charts
Number of People: 2   Time: several days

Grade Level **4**

Materials: Paper and pencil, chart paper

Description: Have your child keep track of the time he spends on activities in a 24-hour period. How many hours does he spend sleeping, playing, going to school, eating, or engaging in other activities. On a barchart, chart the time for each. Then compare the time to how it looks on a pie chart. Now try the tracking activity for a week. Is he surprised at the amount of time he sleeps in comparison to the amount of time he plays? What can he learn from the charts? What changes would he make with the use of his time?

MATH LEARNING STANDARD

Mathematics: Operations & Algebraic Thinking

5. Generate a number or shape pattern that follows a given rule. Identify apparent feature as the pattern that was not explicit in the rule itself.

Need a New Computer
Number of People: 2   Time: Several days

Grade Level **4**

Materials: Newspaper ads

Description: When your family needs a new computer, ask your child to do some comparison shopping. Have him to check ads in the newspaper. What are the prices and the guarantees on at least three computers? Then decide which computer is the best value after reviewing several options. Will he set it up for you once you have bought the best one?

MATH LEARNING STANDARD

Mathematics: Number & Operations in Base Ten

2. Read and write multi-digit numbers using base-ten numerals, numbers names, and expan form. Compare two-multi-digit numbers based on meanings of the digits in each place, usin =, and < symbols to record the results of comparisons.

My Dad was a "star" at math.

Round About

Number of People: 2   Time: 15 minutes

Grade Level **4**

Materials: Paper and pencil

Description: Give your child a large number such as 3,472,568. Let him round the number to the nearest ten, hundred, thousand, ten thousand, and hundred thousand. Remember they need to round up when they get halfway to the next number. I used to love to do hard problems with my Dad. It wasn't just the math I enjoyed. I enjoyed spending some time with my Dad.

MATH LEARNING STANDARD

Mathematics: Number & Operations in Base Ten

3. Use place value understanding to round multi-digit whole numbers to any place.

What we learned today...

_____

_____

_____

_____

_____

_____

_____

 You could spend your saved money on "STARburst" candies.

Newspaper Shopping
Number of People: 2   Time: 30 minutes   Grade Level **4**

Materials: Shopping list, grocery section of the newspaper

Description: Give your child a shopping list, a budget, and the grocery section of your newspaper. Let him find the items on the list in the ads and calculate how much they will cost. What is the total amount? Can he meet the budget? If not, what will he eliminate? If he betters the budget, on what will you spend the saved money?

MATH LEARNING STANDARD

Mathematics: Number & Operations in Base Ten

4. Fluently add and subtract multi-digit whole numbers using the standard algorithm.

What we learned today...

_____

_____

_____

_____

_____

_____

Drying Your Hair Plus

Number of People: 2   Time: 30 minutes

Grade Level **4**

Materials: Math problems on a sheet of paper, pencil

Description: Drying your hair may not be the time for a great conversation, so have a few math problems handy. Some multiplication problems or a long division problem will work. Give the math problems to your child then see which task gets finished first, his math problems or your hair.

MATH LEARNING STANDARD

Mathematics: Number & Operations in Base Ten

5. Multiply a whole number of up to four digits by a one-digit whole number, and multiply two two-digit number, using strategies based on place value and the properties of operations, illustrate and explain the calculation by using equations, rectangular arrays, and/or area models.

Water Fractions

Number of People: 2   Time: 15 minutes

Grade Level **4**

Materials: Plants, water, measuring cup

Description: While you are watering your plants, ask your child to get a ¾ cup of water for one, ¼ cup for another, and so on. Ask why the plants get the portions they get and what each part is in comparison to the whole cup. The plants are watered and the child learns to use a measuring cup.

MATH LEARNING STANDARD

Mathematics: Number & Operations—Fractions

2. Compare two fractions with different numerators and different denominators. Recognize that comparisons are valid only when the two fractions refer to the same whole.

Trip Addition
Number of People: 2   Time: 20 minutes

Grade Level **4**

Materials: A trip in the car, paper and pencil

Description: Have your child add up the mileage when you are on a trip. Start the mileage counter in your car at zero before you begin your trip. At your first stop, have your child write down the mileage. When you get back in your car, start the counter at zero again. At the second stop, have him write the mileage down again. Now, have him add the first mileage to the second. How far have you come so far? Have him add the miles at every stop. How many miles did you go on the first day? How about the second? How about the fifth? What was the total mileage/of your trip? This activity provides lots of opportunity for multi-digit addition and a great trip as well.

MATH LEARNING STANDARD

Mathematics: Measurement & Data

2. Use the four operations to solve word problems involving distances, intervals of time, liquid volumes, masses of objects, and money, including problems involving simple fractions or decimals, and problems that require expressing measurements given in a larger unit in terms or a smaller unit.

Geometric Design
Number of People: 2+   Time: 15 minutes

Grade Level **4**

Materials: Ruler

Description: Rulers are great for measuring, and they make a great straightedge for drawing a line between two points. Put several points on a piece of paper and let your child draw lines between them. Help him identify when the lines are at angles, parallel or perpendicular.

MATH LEARNING STANDARD

Mathematics: Geometry

1. Draw points, lines, line segments, rays, angles, and perpendicular and parallel lines. Identify them in two-dimensional figures.

((((STAR))))

Parentheses Please

Number of People: 2   Time: 15 minutes

Grade Level **5**

Materials: Paper and pencil

Description: Your child has been doing addition, subtraction, and multiplication for quite a while. Use some of the problems he knows and put them in parentheses. In algebra equations, you calculate the items in parentheses in step 1 and the items outside of the parentheses are in the second step of the problem. For example 2X(4+2)= means add 4+2 first to get 6 then multiply 6 by 2 to equal 12. Kids may not be used to seeing parentheses so give them some practice. How much is (2+2)? How much is (3X2)? How about (5-3)? Try a bunch just so he will get used to those ( ).

MATH LEARNING STANDARD

Mathematics: Operations & Algebraic Thinking

1. Use parentheses, brackets, or braces in numerical expressions, and evaluate expressions with these symbols.

What we learned today...

_____

_____

_____

_____

_____

_____

Imagine yourself as an algebra STAR.

Algebra is Easy
Number of People: 2   Time: 15 minutes

Grade Level **5**

Materials: Paper and pencil

Description: You certainly want your child to think math, especially algebra. Make it easy for both of you. Ask him to write down a problem for you. Say something like, "4 plus 2 multiplied by 3". It will look something like this: (4+2) X 3=. He will need to use parentheses to include all the steps. I am sure you will need several problems solved in the next few months so make sure he's around to help you solve them. Try this real life example: If you want to give four Red Delicious apples and two Golden apples to three different people, how many apples will you need altogether? Write the problem down with parentheses and figure it out. Then share the apples!

MATH LEARNING STANDARD

Mathematics: Operations & Algebraic Thinking

2. Write simple expressions that record calculations with numbers, and interpret numerical expressions without evaluating them.

What we learned today...

___
___
___
___
___
___

Shopping Spree

Number of People: 2   Time: 5 minutes   Grade Level **5**

Materials: Groceries in a cart

Description: While standing in the checkout line, ask your child to estimate how much the groceries in the cart will cost. Some hints may be necessary, such as tomato soup costs 20 cents a can, and you have five cans. Chicken is $1.49 a pound, and the chicken you are buying weighs 3 lbs. 5 oz. Now figure out the total. When you get the bill, see how close he came to the correct cost.

MATH LEARNING STANDARD

Mathematics: Number & Operations in Base Ten

3. Read, write, and compare decimals to thousandths.

Yahtzee

Number of People: 2+   Time: 1 hour   Grade Level **5**

Materials: Yahtzee game

Description: Yahtzee is a fun game that reinforces math skills without a whole lot of pain and effort. Engage the whole family in the game.

MATH LEARNING STANDARD

Mathematics: Number & Operations in Base Ten

5. Fluently multiply multi-digit whole numbers using the standard algorithm.

Recipe Add

Number of People: 2 **Time:** Baking Time **Grade Level:** 5

Materials: A favorite baking recipe

Description: Doubling or tripling a recipe is a great activity for younger ages for math. By the time 5th grade arrives, it will be time to make a recipe and a half. This requires adding 1/2 a cup and 1/4 of a cup. There is 1/8 and 1/4 to add together. Next time try two and a half times the recipe and see what happens. Either plan to freeze a lot or have guests. Maybe just make half next time.

MATH LEARNING STANDARD

Mathematics: Fractions

1. Add and subtract fractions with unlike denominators including mixed numbers by replacing given fractions with equivalent fractions in such a way as to produce an equivalent sum or different of fractions with like denominators.

Time to Go

Number of People: 2 **Time:** 45 minutes **Grade Level:** 5

Materials: Paper and pencil

Description: If your destination is 30 miles away from your home, and the speed limit is 60 miles an hour, ask your child how long it will take to reach your planned location. Next time make it harder by needing to travel 49 miles. Try it again with 72 miles. What if the speed limit is 50 miles per hour? Try several variations. Now convert to kilometers.

MATH LEARNING STANDARD

Mathematics: Measurement and Data

1. Convert among different-sized standard measurement units within a given measurement system, and use these conversions in solving multi-step, real world problems.

What we learned today...

_____
_____
_____
_____
_____
_____
_____

Create your own playbook activities!

Math

Number of People: Time: Grade Level

Materials:

Description:

MATH LEARNING STANDARD

Math

Number of People: Time: Grade Level

Materials:

Description:

MATH LEARNING STANDARD

Create your own playbook activities!

Math
Number of People: Time: Grade Level

Materials:
Description:

MATH LEARNING STANDARD

Math
Number of People: Time: Grade Level

Materials:
Description:

MATH LEARNING STANDARD

SCIENCE

3 – 5

Parent Playbook Activities

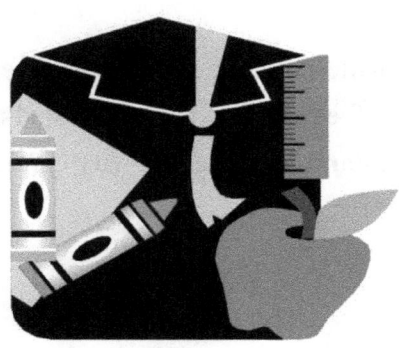

Want to add your favorite activity to the next Parent Playbook?
Use the convenient form in the back of this book or contact the publisher at:

www.familyfriendlyschools.com • www.engagepress.com

By Dr. Joni Samples

SCIENCE LEARNING STANDARDS

SCIENCE LEARNING STANDARDS
Grades 3-5

The purpose of Learning Standards is to enable all students to achieve scientific literacy. The standards used for these activities are a compilation of standards used in districts across the nation.

The K-8 standards are a continuous roadmap of knowledge building one skill upon another. This roadmap tells us how to get to the final destination. Scientific literacy is of increasing importance in our workplace. More and more jobs demand advanced science skills.

The Science Learning Standards provide expectations for the development of student understanding and ability over the course of their K-8 education. We have listed the Science Learning Standards on the following page to help you understand how each activity connects to each standard.

Standard A: Science as Inquiry
- Abilities necessary to do scientific inquiry
- Understanding about scientific inquiry

Standard B: Physical Science
- Properties of objects and materials
- Position and motion of objects
- Light, heat, electricity, and magnetism

Standard C: Life Science
- Characteristics of organisms
- Life cycles of organisms
- Organisms and environment

Standard D: Earth and Space Science
- Properties of earth materials
- Objects in the sky
- Changes in earth and sky

Standard E: Science and Technology
- Abilities of technological design
- Understandings about science and technology
- Abilities to distinguish between natural objects and objects made by humans

Standard F: Science in Personal and Social Perspectives
- Personal Health
- Characteristics and changes in population
- Types of resources
- Change in the environments
- Science and technology in local challenges

Standard G: History and Nature of Science
- Science as a human endeavor

Kitchen Sense

Number of People: 2+   Time: 10-20 minutes   Grade Level **3**

Materials: An apple, a lemon, and a blindfold

Description: Your kids can put their senses to the test in the kitchen. Put a blindfold over their eyes. Have them touch and feel a slice of lemon and a slice of apple. Have them smell both items. Then let them taste each. Next, have them hold their noses and taste. Take off the blindfold and try tasting both holding their nose and not. Do they taste a difference? Describe what happened. Try other items. Is there a taste? When? Why is smell so important?

SCIENCE LEARNING STANDARDS A 1

Essential Skill Activity:
Predict the outcome of a simple investigation and compare the result with the prediction.

 **What we learned today...**

_____

_____

_____

_____

_____

_____

Mixtures and Solutions

Number of People: 2   Time: 20 minutes   Grade Level 3

Materials: Salt, pepper, a cup, and water

Description: Kids can learn the difference between mixtures and solutions by combining a few items in your kitchen. A mixture occurs when you combine two or more items and they both stay the same as they were. Salt and pepper combined together is a mixture. Both the salt and the pepper stay the same. How many mixtures can you find in your kitchen? A solution occurs when two substances are put together and the composition and appearance of the mixture is the same throughout. Salt and water stirred together becomes a solution. What solutions are in your kitchen? See if you can separate the mixtures and solutions. Both can be separated although it may take some work.

SCIENCE LEARNING STANDARDS B 1

Essential Skill Activity:

Students learn that when two or more substances are combined, a new substance may be formed with properties that are different from those of the original materials.

Bubble Time

Number of People: 2+   Time: 15 minutes   Grade Level 3

Materials: Liquid dish soap, water, a shallow tray, and a straw

Description: You have the makings for great bubbles while you are doing the dishes. Put a quart of water and eight tablespoons of dish washing liquid in a shallow tray. This mixture creates a great bubble base. Use a drinking straw to blow into the tray. It will take a little practice, but you can blow some very big bubbles from your tray.

SCIENCE LEARNING STANDARDS B 1

Essential Skill Activity:

Students learn that when two or more substances are combined, a new substance may be formed with properties that are different from those of the original material.

Cleaning Ashes from the Fireplace

Number of People: 2   Time: 15 minutes

Grade Level **3**

Materials: Fireplace, fire

Description: Cleaning out the fireplace is a great time to talk science and safety. Fuel, air, and heat make a fire. How does it happen? What benefits do we get from a fire? What dangers? What are ashes? Where can you put ashes after they cool? What can happen if the ashes are still hot? There are a number of conversations you can have about this topic.

SCIENCE LEARNING STANDARDS B 3

Essential Skill Activity:

Students learn that sources of stored energy take many forms, such as food, fuel, and batteries. Students learn that machines and living things convert stored energy to motion and heat.

Kitchen Matters

Number of People: 2   Time: 30 minutes

Grade Level **3**

Materials: 6 glasses, spoon, water, pencil

Description: Some night, when you are doing the dishes, set out three glasses. In one, put a spoon; in another, pour water; and put nothing in the third. Ask your child if she can see what is in each glass. Take out three cereal bowls. Pour the contents of each of the glasses into the bowls. Does the content assume the shape of the bowl, or does it stay the same? Give each item a name: solid, liquid, or gas. What other solids, liquids, and gases can you find in your kitchen?

SCIENCE LEARNING STANDARDS C 1

Essential Skill Activity:

Students learn that matter has three forms: solid, liquid, and gas.

"Refrigerator Special Effects"
STARring Albert, the Guinea Pig!!

Guinea Pig Pets
Number of People: 2   Time: Several years

Grade Level **3**

Materials: Guinea pig

Description: I have had guinea pigs off and on since I was a kid. A guinea pig makes a great pet for a child. It provides an opportunity to feed and care for an animal as well as a chance to watch a life cycle. Just be careful. Guinea pigs learn to squeak when the refrigerator opens, especially when the open refrigerator means lettuce for them.

SCIENCE LEARNING STANDARDS C 2

Essential Skill Activity:

Students learn that plants and animals have structures that serve different functions in growth, survival, and reproduction.

What we learned today...

_____

_____

_____

_____

_____

_____

Yea! There's just something about sea creatures, especially "star" sea creatures.

Gold Lesson
Number of People: 2   Time: 1 to several days

Grade Level **3**

Materials: A goldfish bowl, goldfish

Description: My daughter had the same goldfish for several years. She fed it, changed its water, rearranged the toys in the bowl, and tried adding several fish friends who didn't manage to outlive the first. Learning about science and responsibility are a nice combination your child can learn from having an inexpensive pet.

SCIENCE LEARNING STANDARDS C 2

Essential Skill Activity:

Students know when the environment changes, some plants and animals survive and reproduce; others die or move to new locations.

What we learned today...

_____

_____

_____

_____

_____

_____

Moonshine

Number of People: 2   Time: A month

Grade Level **3**

Materials: None

Description: Spend some time outdoors or at the window looking at the moon. Have your child keep track of the moon's changes for a month. What happens to the moon? Where do parts of it go? Why do the changes happen? See if the moon looks the same next month during the same time frame.

SCIENCE LEARNING STANDARDS D 2

Essential Skill Activity:

Students learn the way in which the moon's appearance changes during the four-week lunar cycle.

Summer Light

Number of People: 2   Time: 20 minutes

Grade Level **3**

Materials: None

Description: Why do we have daylight longer in summer? Talk about those lighter hours with your child while you are enjoying the long summer evenings. What happens in the winter? Where does the sun go in the sky? Why does the position of the sun change?

SCIENCE LEARNING STANDARDS D 2

Essential Skill Activity:

Students learn the position of the sun in the sky changes during the course of the day and from season to season.

Squeaky Hinge

Number of People: 2   Time: 30 minutes

Grade Level **4**

Materials: Squeaky door hinge, oil, water

Description: When a door hinge squeaks, we put a little oil on it. Next time it squeaks ask your child what he would need to do to fix the squeak. What would happen if you put water on it? How about Jell-O? Let your child oil the hinge next time and be sure to ask him why it works. If he doesn't know, you may want to talk about oil and lubricants.

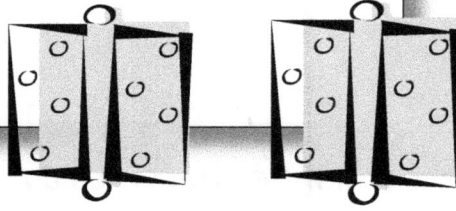

SCIENCE LEARNING STANDARDS A 2

Essential Skill Activity:

Students learn how to make and defend predictions based on cause-and-effect relationships.

Summer Wading

Number of People: 2   Time: 30 minutes

Grade Level **4**

Materials: Wading pool, gallon jug, bucket

Description: A wading pool needs to be filled before anyone can use it. Ask your child how many gallons of water it takes to fill the pool. Give him a gallon jug and let him fill the pool. If it's too slow, give him a four-gallon bucket. How does he figure out how many gallons are in the pool?

SCIENCE LEARNING STANDARDS B 1

Essential Skill Activity:

Measure and estimate the weight, length, or volume of objects.

It's "star"tling how much rain can come from one storm.

Rain Gauge
Number of People: 2   Time: An hour or so

Grade Level **4**

Materials: Coffee can, ruler

Description: Put a coffee can outside to catch rain. How much rain do you think might come from a storm? Measure the rain in the can with a ruler after the storm is over. How much rain did you get? Did it seem like the storm brought more rain than the gauge showed? How can you predict how much rain will come from each storm? How do you think the weather forecaster knows?

SCIENCE LEARNING STANDARDS B 1

Essential Skill Activity:

Measure and estimate the weight, length, or volume of objects.

What we learned today...

___
___
___
___
___
___

Could this be a "star"chy recipe?

Science Cakes
Number of People: 2   Time: 60 minutes

Grade Level **4**

Materials: Cake mix ingredients

Description: Bake several cakes from scratch. Put all the correct ingredients in one cake. In others, leave out one ingredient: the egg, the oil, the baking powder. Bake each cake and observe. See if you can predict what will happen. What happens to each? What chemical reaction is required from each ingredient? You might want to eat only one of the cakes.

SCIENCE LEARNING STANDARDS B 1

Essential Skill Activity:

Students learn how chemical reactions affect atoms.

What we learned today...

_____

_____

_____

_____

_____

_____

Creating a Charge

Number of People: 2   Time: 30 minutes

Grade Level: 4

Materials: A balloon and some Styrofoam packing pieces or a Styrofoam cup broken into pieces

Description: Blow up a balloon and have your child rub it against his hair. Then move the balloon near pieces of Styrofoam. What happens? Why did the pieces move? Which way did they go? See if you can find information on the Internet to tell you what happened and why.

SCIENCE LEARNING STANDARDS B 3

Essential Skill Activity:

Students will learn electrically charged objects attract or repel each other.

Electric Hair

Number of People: 2   Time: 10 minutes

Grade Level: 4

Materials: Balloon

Description: Blow up a balloon and rub it across your child's hair. Ask him what happens. How does his hair feel? What happens to his hair? It is static electricity he is feeling. Check your science book or the Internet for information about static electricity.

SCIENCE LEARNING STANDARDS B 3

Essential Skill Activity:

Students will learn electrically charged objects attract or repel each other.

Salsa

Number of People: 2   Time: Several months   Grade Level **4**

Materials: Tomato, green onion, and herb plants

Description: Plants are the primary source of matter and energy for animals within a food chain. Grow a few plants in your garden to help start the food chain. Tomatoes, green onions, and herbs are easy to grow and are wonderful when put together to make salsa. Just make sure you and your child get the results of the plants rather than the tomato worms or other local varmints. They are part of the food chain too.

SCIENCE LEARNING STANDARDS C 2

Essential Skill Activity:

Kids learn plants are the primary source of matter and energy entering most food chains.

Seed Study

Number of People: 1+   Time: Dinner time   Grade Level **4**

Materials: Lima beans

Description: Next time you fix lima beans for dinner, do a little seed dissection first. Soaking the beans for a day in a pan of water makes the process easier. Take the seed coat off and then split the seed in half. Talk about what is inside. Plant a couple of the ones you don't dissect and see what else happens.

SCIENCE LEARNING STANDARDS C 2

Essential Skill Activity:

Students will learn that plants are the primary source of matter and energy entering most food chains.

Fungus can "star"t on any food you leave out too long.

Growing Fungi
Number of People: 2   Time: Several days

Grade Level **4**

Materials: A slice of bread, a slice of fruit, two saucers, a paper towel, notebook, and a pencil

Description: Let your child dampen a paper towel. Put a slice of bread on a saucer. Then cover the bread with the dampened paper towel. Have him put the saucer in a dark, warm place. Put a slice of fruit on a saucer and place it in a dark, warm place as well. Have him check the bread and fruit daily to see what happens. Keep a record of observations in a notebook to show the progress of fungus growth. What does the bread look like in four days? How about the fruit? What is growing on each? Which grows faster? Why? On occasion, you may find things like this growing on other foods in your refrigerator. Those can be thrown away. After a couple of weeks, you can throw your experiment away too.

SCIENCE LEARNING STANDARDS C 2

Essential Skill Activity:

Students know decomposers, including many fungi, insects, and microorganisms, recycle matter from dead plants and animals.

What we learned today...

_____

_____

_____

_____

_____

_____

_____

The inside of a geode looks like "star" shine to me.

Mineral Sales
Number of People: 2   Time: an hour or so   Grade Level **4**

Materials: Minerals or information about minerals such as quartz, calcite, feldspar, or mica

Description: Have your child create a script for a commercial advertising a wonderful mineral. He needs to provide information about the mineral. What color is it? What uses does it have? Where can it be found? Have him check the Internet or other sources to find information for his advertisement.

SCIENCE LEARNING STANDARDS D 1

Essential Skill Activity:

Students learn how to identify different kinds of rocks – igneous, sedimentary, and metamorphic.

What we learned today...

_____
_____
_____
_____
_____
_____

Breaking Rocks

Number of People: 2   Time: 15 minutes   Grade Level **4**

Materials: Rocks, moving water

Description: Water reshapes the land by taking it away from some places and depositing it as pebbles, sand, silt, and mud in other places. Rocks change shape in the process. In moving water, the sharp edges of a small rock erode to form smooth pebbles. Have your child pick up several rocks near a creek bed. From its physical features, can you tell if the rock has been underwater? Start a collection and see how many different kinds of rocks you can find.

SCIENCE LEARNING STANDARDS D 3

Essential Skill Activity:

Students learn that moving water erodes landforms, reshaping the land by taking it away from some places and depositing it as pebbles, sand, silt, and mud in other places.

What we learned today...

_____

_____

_____

_____

_____

_____

_____

Starch Detective

Number of People: 2   Time: 20 minutes

Grade Level **5**

Materials: Food items such as a piece of bread, slices of apple, orange, banana, cheese, and potato, milk, pineapple juice, etc.; a bottle of tincture of iodine, a medicine dropper

Description: We are all concerned about what we eat these days, but we may not know a great deal about many foods. Some foods have high starch content. Which foods do you eat that have starch in them? We can find out which foods are starchy by dropping one drop of iodine on each of the items described above in the materials list. A food that contains starch will turn the iodine a dark purple-blue color. Have your child check her favorite foods to see if they contain starch.

SCIENCE LEARNING STANDARDS A 2

Essential Skill Activity:

Plan and conduct a simple investigation based on a question, and write instructions others can follow to carry out the procedure.

Cabbage Experiments

Number of People: 2   Time: 15 minutes

Grade Level **5**

Materials: Plastic cups, red cabbage, hot water, lemon juice, baking soda

Description: Some evening while making dinner, put some red cabbage in a plastic cup. Add hot water. The water will turn blue. You now have an acid base indicator. Separate the blue water into two cups and put some lemon juice in one and baking soda in the other. What happens? What has an acid base? Why? Once more, science is in the kitchen.

SCIENCE LEARNING STANDARDS B 1

Essential Skill Activity:

Students learn how chemical reactions affect atoms.

Oil and Water

Number of People: 2 Time: 15 minutes Grade Level 5

Materials: Measuring cup, water, oil, cookie mix

Description: Someday when you are frying food, have your child get both the oil you need and a 1/4 cup of water. Put the two together. What happens? Why don't they mix? Why does the oil stay on top? Oil is less dense than water so it floats. Finish cooking. Don't forget to add your oil. While the food is frying, let him look for other items that might be less dense than water.

SCIENCE LEARNING STANDARDS B 1

Essential Skill Activity:

Students learn that during chemical reactions the atoms in the reactants rearrange to form products with different properties.

Pinwheels

Number of People: 1 or 2 Time: 30 minutes Grade Level 5

Materials: Pinwheel

Description: It is possible to see the path of air currents when smoke blows from a chimney or you blow air on the steam from a cup of hot cocoa. When you blow on a pinwheel the air current cannot be seen, but you can see the pinwheel move. The harder you blow the faster the pinwheel goes. When you blow softly, you have little movement. When you stop blowing, the pinwheel stops. Discuss the movement of large masses of air when fog or clouds form. What makes air move?

SCIENCE LEARNING STANDARDS D 2

Essential Skill Activity:

Students learn that water vapor in the air moves from one place to another and can form fog or clouds, which are tiny droplets of water or ice, and can fall to earth as rain, hail, sleet, or snow.

Will it be a "star"ry night?

Weather or Not

Number of People: 2   Time: Several weeks or so

Grade Level **5**

Materials: Daily newspaper or computer with Internet access

Description: Have your child check the weather daily. Have him keep a weather chart so he can tell what the trends are. It is possible to generate many discussions about seasons, what clothes to wear, and when to plant rutabagas.

SCIENCE LEARNING STANDARDS D 3 & F 5

Essential Skill Activity:

Record data by using appropriate graphic representations (including charts, graphs, and labeled diagrams) and make inferences based on those data.

What we learned today...

___
___
___
___
___
___

Create your own playbook activities!

Science
Number of People: Time: Grade Level

Materials:
Description:

COMMON SCIENCE STANDARD

Science
Number of People: Time: Grade Level

Materials:
Description:

COMMON SCIENCE STANDARD

Create your own playbook activities!

Science

Number of People: Time: Grade Level

Materials:

Description:

COMMON SCIENCE STANDARD

Science

Number of People: Time: Grade Level

Materials:

Description:

COMMON SCIENCE STANDARD

HISTORY

3 – 5

Parent Playbook Activities

Want to add your favorite activity to the next Parent Playbook?
Use the convenient form in the back of this book or contact the publisher at:

www.familyfriendlyschools.com • www.engagepress.com

By Dr. Joni SamplesHistory Learning Standards

LEARNING STANDARDS
HISTORY/SOCIAL STUDIES
Grades 3-5

The purpose of the History/Social Studies Learning Standards is to enable all students to achieve an understanding of history. The following standards for History/Social Studies are a compilation of standards being used in districts across the nation.

The K-8 standards are a continuous roadmap of knowledge building one skill upon another. This roadmap tells us how to get to the final destination.

The History/Social Studies Learning Standards provide expectations for the development of student understanding and ability over the course of their K-8 education.

We have listed History/Social Studies Learning Standards on the following pages to help you understand how each activity connects to each standard. Also included are the Historical Thinking Standards to help create thoughtful reflection of historic events.

HISTORY
Grades 3-5

Standards in history make explicit the goals that all students should have the opportunity to acquire. In history, standards are of two types:

1. Historical thinking skills. Being able to think enables students to evaluate evidence, compare and analyze, be able to explain, and put together sound historical arguments and evaluate and make informed decisions.

2. Historical understandings. This defines what students should know about the history of their nation and of the world. Students learn this through studying the social, political, scientific/technological, economic, and cultural (philosophical/religious/aesthetic) records. These records also provide students the historical perspectives required to analyze contemporary issues and problems confronting citizens today.

Both the World and United States Standards are printed for your information as well as the Historical Thinking Standards.

A NOTE ABOUT THE HISTORY SECTION

The standards in History look very different from other standards listed in this Playbook. Why? Well, the study of history involves much more than the passive absorption of facts, dates, names, and places. History is in essence a process of reasoning based on evidence from the past. This reasoning must be grounded in the careful gathering, weighing and sifting of information such as names, dates, places, ideas, and events. However, the process does not stop here. Real historical understanding requires students to think through cause-and-effect relationships, to reach sound historical interpretations, and to conduct historical inquiries and research leading to the knowledge on which informed decisions in contemporary life can be based.

History itself is a highly integrative field, engaging students in studies not only of the people and of events in their community, state, nation, and world, but opening as well the study of the geographic places in which these events occurred. It includes the ideas, beliefs, and values that influenced how people acted in their daily lives; the rules, laws, and institutions they established and lived by; the oral traditions and the literature, music, art, architecture, and dance they created; and the technological and scientific developments they invented, or adopted, in their quest to improve daily life. In short, studies in history necessarily include geographic, economic, political, social, and scientific studies, as well as studies in the arts.

Historical thinking and understanding do not develop independently of one another. Historical thinking skills enable students to evaluate evidence, develop comparative and causal analyses, interpret the historical record, and construct sound historical arguments and perspectives on which informed decisions in contemporary life can be based. Historical understandings define what students should know about the history of their nation and of the world. These understandings also provide students the historical perspectives required to analyze contemporary issues and problems confronting citizens today.

In the History/Social Studies section of your Parent Playbook the History/Social Studies Learning Standard is listed below the activity. The Thinking Standard is listed by number and you may refer back to the beginning of the chapter for the actual standard.

HISTORY LEARNING STANDARDS
Grades 3-4

Standard 1
Understands family life now and in the past, and family life in various places long ago

Standard 2
Understands the history of the local community and how communities in North America varied long ago

Standard 3
Understands the people, events, problems, and ideas that were significant in creating the history of their State

Standard 4
Understands how democratic values came to be, and how they have been exemplified by people, events, and symbols

Standard 5
Understands the causes and nature of movements of large groups of people into and within the United States, now and long ago

Standard 6
Understands the folklore and other cultural contributions from various regions of the United States and how they helped to form a national heritage

Standard 7
Understands selected attributes and historical developments of societies in Africa, the Americas, Asia, and Europe

Standard 8
Understands major discoveries in science and technology, some of their social and economic effects, and the major scientists and inventors responsible for them

UNITED STATES HISTORY LEARNING STANDARD
Grade 5

Era 1: Three Worlds Meet (Beginnings to 1620)
Standard 1: Comparative characteristics of societies in the Americas, Western Europe, and Western Africa that increasingly interacted after 1450
Standard 2: How early European exploration and colonization resulted in cultural and ecological interactions among previously unconnected peoples

Era 2: Colonization and Settlement (1585-1763)
Standard 1: Why the Americas attracted Europeans, why they brought enslaved Africans to their colonies, and how Europeans struggled for control of North America and the Caribbean
Standard 2: How political, religious, and social institutions emerged in the English colonies
Standard 3: How the values and institutions of European economic life took root in the colonies, and how slavery reshaped European and African life in the Americas

Era 3: Revolution and the New Nation (1754-1820's)
Standard 1: The causes of the American Revolution, the ideas and interests involved in forging the revolutionary movement, and the reasons for the American victory
Standard 2: The impact of the American Revolution on politics, economy, and society
Standard 3: The institutions and practices of government created during the Revolution and how they were revised between 1787 and 1815 to create the foundation of the American political system based on the U.S. Constitution and the Bill of Rights

Era 4: Expansion and Reform (1801-1861)
Standard 1: United States territorial expansion between 1801 and 1861, and how it affected relations with external powers and Native Americans
Standard 2: How the industrial revolution, increasing immigration, the rapid expansion of slavery, and the westward movement changed the lives of Americans and led toward regional tensions
Standard 3: The extension, restriction, and reorganization of political democracy after 1800
Standard 4: The sources and character of cultural, religious, and social reform movements in the antebellum period

Era 5: Civil War and Reconstruction (1850-1877)
Standard 1: The causes of the Civil War
Standard 2: The course and character of the Civil War and its effects on the American people

Standard 3: How various reconstruction plans succeeded or failed

Era 6: The Development of the Industrial United States (1870-1900)
Standard 1: How the rise of corporations, heavy industry, and mechanized farming transformed the American people
Standard 2: Massive immigration after 1870 and how new social patterns, conflicts, and ideas of national unity developed amid growing cultural diversity
Standard 3: The rise of the American Labor Movement and how political issues reflected social and economic changes
Standard 4: Federal Indian policy and United States foreign policy after the Civil War

Era 7: The Emergence of Modern America (1890-1930)
Standard 1: How Progressives and others addressed problems of industrial capitalism, urbanization, and political corruption
Standard 2: The changing role of the United States in world affairs through World War I
Standard 3: How the United States changed from the end of World War I to the eve of the Great Depression

Era 8: The Great Depression and World War II (1929-1945)
Standard 1: The causes of the Great Depression and how it affected American society
Standard 2: How the New Deal addressed the Great Depression, transformed American federalism, and initiated the welfare state
Standard 3: The causes and course of World War II, the character of the war at home and abroad, and its reshaping of the U.S. role in world affairs

Era 9: Postwar United States (1945 to early 1970s)
Standard 1: the economic boom and social transformation of postwar United States
Standard 2: How the Cold War and conflicts in Korea and Vietnam influenced domestic and international politics
Standard 3: Domestic policies after World War II
Standard 4: The struggle for racial and gender equality and the extension of civil liberties

Era 10: Contemporary United States (1968 to the present)
Standard 1: Recent developments in foreign and domestic politics
Standard 2: Economic, social, and cultural developments in contemporary United States

HISTORICAL THINKING STANDARDS
Grades 3-5

STANDARD 1

The student thinks chronologically: Therefore, the student is able to:

A. Distinguish between past, present, and future time.
B. Identify the temporal structure of a historical narrative or story: its beginning, middle, and end (the latter defined as the outcome of a particular beginning).
C. Establish temporal order in constructing their [students'] own historical narratives: working forward from some beginning through its development, to some end or outcome; working backward from some issue, problem, or event to explain its origins and its development over time.
D. Measure and calculate calendar time by days, weeks, months, years, decades, centuries and millennia, from fixed points of the calendar system: BC (before Christ) and AD (Anno Domini, "in the year of our Lord") in the Gregorian calendar and the contemporary secular designation for these same dates, BCE (before the Common Era) and CE (in the Common Era); and compare with the fixed points of other calendar systems such as the Roman (753BC, the founding of the city of Rome) and the Muslim (622 AD, the hegira).
E. Interpret data presented in time lines by designating appropriate equidistant intervals of time and recording events according to the temporal order in which they occurred.
F. Reconstruct patterns of historical succession and duration in which historical developments have unfolded, and apply them to explain historical continuity and change.
G. Compare alternative models for periodization by identifying the organizing principles on which each is based.

STANDARD 2:

The student comprehends a variety of historical sources: Therefore, the student is able to:

A. Identify the author or source of the historical document or narrative.
B. Reconstruct the literal meaning of a historical passage by identifying who was involved, what happened, where it happened, what events led to these developments, and what consequences or outcomes followed.
C. Identify the central question(s) the historical narrative addresses and the purpose, perspective, or point of view from which it has been constructed.
D. Differentiate between historical facts and historical interpretations but acknowledge that the two

are related; that the facts the historian reports are selected and reflect therefore the historian's judgment of what is most significant about the past.

E. Read historical narratives imaginatively, taking into account what the narrative reveals of the humanity of the individuals and groups involved – their probable values, outlook, motives, hopes, fears, strengths, and weaknesses.

F. Appreciate historical perspectives – the ability (a) describing the past on its own terms, through the eyes and experiences of those who were there, as revealed through their literature, diaries, letters, debates, arts, artifacts, and the like; (b) considering the historical context in which the event unfolded – the values, outlook, options, and contingencies of that time and place; and (c) avoiding "present-mindedness," judging the past solely in terms of present-day norms and values.

G. Draw upon data in historical maps in order to obtain or clarify information on the geographic setting in which the historical event occurred, its relative and absolute location, the distances and directions involved, the natural and man-made features of the place, and critical relationships in the spatial distributions of those features and the historical event occurring there.

H. Utilize visual and mathematical data presented in graphs, including charts, tables, pie and bar graphs, flow charts, Venn diagrams, and other graphic organizers to clarify, illustrate, or elaborate upon information presented in the historical narrative.

I. Draw upon the visual, literary, and musical sources including: (a) photographs, paintings, cartoons, and architectural drawings; (b) novels, poetry, and plays; and (c) folk, popular, and classical music, to clarify, illustrate, or elaborate upon information presented in the historical narrative.

STANDARD 3:
The student engages in historical analysis and interpretation: therefore, the student is able to:

A. Compare and contrast differing sets of ideas, values, personalities, behaviors, and institutions by identifying likenesses and differences.

B. Consider multiple perspectives of various peoples in the past by demonstrating their differing motives, beliefs, interests, hopes, and fears.

C. Analyze cause-and-effect relationships bearing in mind multiple causation including (a) the importance of the individual in history; (b) the influence of ideas, human interests, and beliefs; and (c) the role of chance, the accidental and the irrational.

D. Draw comparisons across eras and regions in order to define enduring issues as well as large-scale or long-term developments that transcend regional and temporal boundaries.

E. Distinguish between unsupported expressions of opinion and informed hypotheses grounded in historical evidence.

F. Compare competing historical narratives.

G. Challenge arguments of historical inevitability by formulating examples of historical contingency, of how different choices could have led to different consequences.

H. Hold interpretations of history as tentative, subject to changes as new information is uncovered, new voices heard, and new interpretations broached.

I. Evaluate major debates among historians concerning alternative interpretations of the past.
J. Hypothesize the influence of the past, including both the limitations and opportunities made possible by past decisions.

STANDARD 4:

The student conducts historical research: Therefore, the student is able to:

A. Formulate historical questions from encounters with historical documents, eyewitness accounts, letters, diaries, artifacts, photos, historical sites, art, architecture, and other records from the past.
B. Obtain historical data from a variety of sources, including: library and museum collections, historic sites, historical photos, journals, diaries, eyewitness accounts, newspapers, and the like; documentary films, oral testimony from living witnesses, censuses, tax records, city directories, statistical compilations, and economic indicators.
C. Interrogate historical data by uncovering the social, political, and economic context in which it was created; testing the data source for its credibility, authority, authenticity, internal consistency and completeness; and detecting and evaluating bias, distortion, and propaganda by omission, suppression, or invention of facts.
D. Identify the gaps in the available records and marshal contextual knowledge and perspectives of the time and place in order to elaborate imaginatively upon the evidence, fill in the gaps deductively, and construct a sound historical interpretation.
E. Employ quantitative analysis in order to explore such topics as changes in family size and composition, migration patterns, wealth distribution, and changes in the economy.
F. Support interpretations with historical evidence in order to construct closely reasoned arguments rather than facile opinions.

STANDARD 5:

The student engages in historical issues-analysis and decision making: Therefore, the student is able to:

A. Identify issues and problems in the past and analyze the interests, values, perspectives, and points of view of those involved in the situation.
B. Marshal evidence of antecedent circumstances and current factors contributing to contemporary problems and alternative courses of action.
C. Identify relevant historical antecedents and differentiate from those that are inappropriate and irrelevant to contemporary issues.
D. Evaluate alternative courses of action, keeping in mind the information available at the time, in terms of ethical considerations, the interests of those affected by the decision, and the long- and short-term consequences of each.
E. Formulate a position or course of action on an issue by identifying the nature of the problem, analyzing the underlying factors contributing to the problem, and choosing a plausible solution from a choice of carefully evaluated options.
F. Evaluate the implementation of a decision by analyzing the interests it served; estimating the position, power, and priority of each player involved; assessing the ethical dimensions of the decision; and evaluating its costs and benefits from a variety of perspectives.

Local Native American Folklore
Number of People: 2   Time: An hour or so   Grade Level 3

Materials: Access to Native American history

Description: Many communities have a Native American tribe nearby. Let your child investigate the local tribal customs, beliefs, and folklore. What is the history of the tribe? How have they changed? What are today's customs?

HISTORY LEARNING STANDARDS 1 & 2

Standard 1: Understands family life now and in the past, and family life in various places long ago.

Standard 2: Understands the history of the local community and how communities in North America varied long ago.

HISTORICAL THINKING STANDARD 2 G

School as Work
Number of People: 2+   Time: A school year   Grade Level 3

Materials: Work and school sites

Description: We told our children going to school was their job. We went to an office to work, and they went to school to work. Let your child visit your work sometimes. You need to visit their workday at school. There are always things to talk about at the dinner table when everyone has had a busy day.

HISTORY LEARNING STANDARDS 2 & 3

Standard 1: Understands family life now and in the past, and family life in various places long ago.

Standard 3: Understands the people, events, problems, and ideas that were significant in creating the history of their State.

HISTORICAL THINKING STANDARD 3 A

You Are There and You Are a STAR.

You Are There		Grade Level **3**
Number of People: 2	Time: 30 minutes	

Materials: Book or the Internet for research

Description: Your child may not know about an old television program titled, "You Are There." The program was on TV for quite a number of years and featured a roving reporter who visited historic events as they happened. Actors portrayed the people of the time. The program highlighted historical figures like Thomas Jefferson during important events such as the signing of the Declaration of Independence or it highlighted common people that may have been in Ford's Theater at the assassination of Abraham Lincoln. The reporter interviewed people at the scene and, voila, "You Are There." Have your child pick a time in your local history and interview you as if you were there at the time. Then turn the tables. You interview him about a time in your city he chooses. Just know that "You Are There."

HISTORY LEARNING STANDARDS 2 & 5

Standard 2: Understands the history of the local community and how communities in North American varied long ago.

Standard 5: Understands the causes and nature of movements of large groups of people into and within the United States, now and long ago.

HISTORICAL THINKING STANDARD 4 A, B, & C

What we learned today...

_____

_____

_____

_____

_____

_____

Local History	Grade Level **3**
Number of People: 2 Time: Several days	

Materials: Areas of history in your town

Description: Your town has a history. Let your child find out about your town's beginnings, its settlers, and the people of the region. A visit to a local museum, a trip to the newspaper office, or a tour of government buildings could provide a flavor of what it was like to live in your town 100 years ago. We have several places in our town with pictures of old buildings and events. What is in your town?

HISTORY STANDARD 3

Standard 3: Understands the people, events, problems, and ideas that were significant in creating the history of their State.

HISTORICAL THINKING STANDARD 3 A, B, & C

What we learned today...

_____

_____

_____

_____

_____

_____

Bridging Gaps
Number of People: 2   Time: A few minutes   Grade Level 3

Materials: A trip that includes crossing a river by bridge

Description: Before reaching a bridge, have some discussion with your child about why you need a bridge over a river. What other ways could you cross a river if the bridge wasn't there? How did people cross rivers before bridges were built? Ask many questions just for fun. When you have exhausted your questions, talk about the communities on either side of the bridge. Who used to live there? How did the communities develop? How have they changed? Did the bridge make a difference to the communities?

HISTORY STANDARD 3

Standard 3: Understands the people, events, problems, and ideas that were significant in creating the history of their state.

HISTORICAL THINKING STANDARDS 5 A, D, & E

Name that Park
Number of People: 2   Time: 30 minutes   Grade Level 3

Materials: Books or the Internet for research

Description: There are 48 National Parks in the United States. Let your child select one of those parks, and describe it until you can guess which one it is and where it is located. Plan to visit one or more of the National Parks. Then you can discuss why it might be important to take care of such an important part of our country.

HISTORY LEARNING STANDARDS 4 & 6

Standard 4: Understands how democratic values came to be, and how they have been exemplified by people, events, and symbols.

Standard 5: Understands the causes and nature of movements of large groups of people in and within the United States, now and long ago.

HISTORICAL THINKING STANDARDS 2 G, H, & I

Exploring Explorers
Number of People: 2   Time: 15 minutes

Grade Level **3**

Materials: Book or the Internet for research

Description: Have your child pick one explorer who visited your town or state. Do a little research to see what she can find out about her chosen explorer including birthplace, family background, failures, successes, culture, and religious beliefs. Have a chat about what effect their lives and their discoveries have on us today.

HISTORY LEARNING STANDARDS 5 & 6

Standard 5: Understands the causes and nature of movements of large groups of people into and within the United States, now and long ago.

Standard 6: Understands the folklore and other cultural contributions from various regions of the United States and how they helped to form a national heritage.

HISTORICAL THINKING STANDARDS 4 A & B

Exploring Is Exploring
Number of People: 2   Time: 20 minutes

Grade Level **3**

Materials: None

Description: Have a chat with your child about exploring space. Is space exploration like the exploration of the New World discovered by Columbus? How? What geographical features would you find on a planet or the moon? What do you think our historic explorers felt like when they found deserts, mountains, oceans or other earth forms? What landforms did they find when they explored places around where you live?

HISTORY STANDARD 8

Standard 8: Understands major discoveries in science and technology, some of their social and economic effects, and the major scientists and inventors responsible for them.

HISTORICAL THINKING STANDARD 3 B & 2 I

Historically speaking who are the "stars" in your community?

Picture This

Number of People: 2 or more   Time: An hour

Grade Level **4**

Materials: Brochures about your state

Description: Help your kids make a historic scrapbook on the founding of their state. Gather brochures from stops you make during a road trip or get them from your local chamber of commerce. Have your children circle dates for an event as they find it or look it up on the Internet. Let them arrange the pictures for the scrapbook from oldest events to the most recent. They can practice writing skills if you ask for a written description of each picture.

HISTORY LEARNING STANDARDS 1, 2, & 3

Standard 1: Understands family life now and in the past, and family life in various places long ago.

Standard 2: Understands the history of the local community and how communities in North America varied long ago.

Standard 3: Understands the people, events, problems, and ideas that were significant in creating the history of their State.

HISTORICAL THINKING STANDARDS 1 A & 2 F

What we learned today...

_____

_____

_____

_____

_____

_____

Can you also map a road to the beach?
Starfish love beach trips.

Build a New Road

Number of People: 2   Time: Several hours

Grade Level **4**

Materials: Maps for your vacation

Description: Sometimes getting from one spot to another takes a long time. Sometimes when you go on vacation, it seems to take forever to get from home to your favorite destination. Make the trip more interesting by having your child devise a new route. What other ways could your family travel that is shorter? If an alternative road does not exist, is it possible to build one? What kind of terrain would you have to go through? What mountains, rivers, plains or other areas would you have to traverse? How much shorter would the new route be? What would be in the way? Is it possible to build this new route? Why or why not?

HISTORY STANDARD 3

Standard 3: Understands the people, events, problems, and ideas that were significant in creating the history of their State.

HISTORICAL THINKING STANDARDS 4 A & B

What we learned today...

_____
_____
_____
_____
_____
_____

Dust Bowl Immigration
Number of People: 2   Time: An afternoon

Grade Level **4**

Materials: Information from books or the Internet, paper, pencil

Description: The drought and farming practices in the area called the Dust Bowl resulted in thousands of people having to leave their homes. Ask your child to find out what region of the United States was known as the Dust Bowl, what caused the Dust Bowl, and why the people had to leave. Ask her to write a story about what it would have been like to be one of the Dust Bowl immigrants.

HISTORY STANDARD 3

Standard 3: Understands the people, events, problems, and ideas that were significant in creating the history of their state.
HISTORICAL THINKING STANDARDS 4 A & 4 B

Know Your Representatives
Number of People: 2   Time: A few hours

Grade Level **4**

Materials: List of State officials and representatives

Description: Do you know your state's representatives in Congress? Who are your Senators? How many representatives does your state have? Who is your Governor? What are the significant issues that are facing your state? Gather all the information and play "20 Questions" with your family.

HISTORY LEARNING STANDARDS 3 & 4

Standard 3: Understands the people, events, problems, and ideas that were significant in creating the history of their State.

Standard 4: Understands how democratic values came to be, and how they have been exemplified by people, events, and symbols.
HISTORICAL THINKING STANDARD 5 F

"Give Us Statehood"

Number of People: 2 or more Time: Several days Grade Level 4

Materials: Book or the Internet for research

Description: Ask your child to look around the community to see what influences still exist from the founding fathers of the state. Have him find out how statehood made a difference. Is your state better being a part of the United States? What advantages do we have being one of the United States?

HISTORY LEARNING STANDARDS 3, 5, & 6

Standard 3: Understands the people, events, problems, and ideas that were significant in creating the history of their State.

Standard 5: Understands the causes and nature of movements of large groups of people into and within the United States, now and long ago.

Standard 6: Understands the folklore and other cultural contributions from various regions of the United States and how they helped to form a national heritage.

HISTORICAL THINKING STANDARD 1 A

Your State's Historians

Number of People: 2 Time: Several hours Grade Level 4

Materials: History books, the Internet, or a trip to Sutter's Fort

Description: Sutter found the first gold in California. Ask your child to investigate a special event that happened in your state. Have her learn about the event and about the exploits of the people involved. How did the event change the history of your state?

HISTORY LEARNING STANDARDS 5 & 6

Standard 5: Understands the causes and nature of movements of large groups of people into and within the United States, now and long ago.

Standard 6: Understands the folklore and other cultural contributions from various regions of the United States and how they helped to form a national heritage.

HISTORICAL THINKING STANDARDS 3 E & 4 C

It "star"tles me to know how much water we use every day.
Did you know Starfish like salt in their water?

Water, Water Everywhere

Number of People: 2   Time: An hour

Grade Level 4

Materials: Books or the Internet

Description: Water has always been a big topic of discussion in for most states. Water was important in our history, and it is now. As towns have grown up, the people in the towns need a great deal of water to live. Ask your child to find out where water comes from, how it gets from place to place, and why it is important today. Have him come up with a way to get water to your house.

HISTORY STANDARD 8

Standard 8: Understands major discoveries in science and technology, some of their social and economic effects, and the major scientists and inventors responsible for them.

HISTORICAL THINKING STANDARDS 5 A & 5 D

What we learned today...

_____
_____
_____
_____
_____
_____
_____

If your put a letter in a bottle, and threw it in the sea, even Starfish could read it!

Historic Letter

Number of People: 2   Time: 45 minutes

Grade Level **5**

Materials: Paper and pencil

Description: Ask your kids to write a special letter to you. Tell them you would like them to write the letter as if they were someone coming over with Columbus. Perhaps you would like to get a letter from someone in the Revolutionary War, or maybe a letter from someone in the Lewis and Clark Expedition. You can pick almost anytime in history, and they can create a fascinating story for you.

U.S. HISTORY STANDARD – ERA 1, STANDARD 1; ERA 2, STANDARD 2

Era 1, Standard 1: Comparative characteristics of societies in the Americas, Western Europe, and Western Africa that increasingly interacted after 1450.

Era 2, Standard 2: How political, religious, and social institutions emerged in the English colonies

HISTORICAL THINKING STANDARD 2 B

What we learned today...

_____

_____

_____

_____

_____

_____

Tell the Truth
Number of People: 2   Time: 45+ minutes   Grade Level **5**

Materials: Paper and pencil or computer, Internet access

Description: Ask your child if Christopher Columbus was the first and only one to discover North America. Who was Amerigo Vespucci? Who was Leif Ericsson? What did he do? Were there others who found America? What technological equipment did these men use as they navigated the seas? The Internet is a good place to do some checking on historical stories. After your child confirms or denies the facts about America's history, have him rewrite history in his words with the facts he found.

U.S. HISTORY STANDARD - ERA 1, STANDARD 2

Era 1, Standard 2: How early European exploration and colonization resulted in cultural and ecological interactions among previously unconnected peoples.

HISTORICAL THINKING STANDARDS 4 A, 4 B, & 4 C

What State Am I?
Number of People: 2   Time: An hour or more   Grade Level **5**

Materials: An encyclopedia, map and/or the Internet for research

Description: "What State I am" is a game. Have your child pretend to be one of the states. You can begin with the first thirteen colonies—our first states. You will have to guess which one. Your child will need to know a little about the state to be able to give you clues. For example, what the state looks like, who lived there, what famous person came from there, or what special event took place there. You can decide which states to choose depending on what part of history your child is studying at the time. The states of the Lewis and Clark Expedition or the states that came out of the Louisiana Purchase are other possibilities.

U.S. HISTORY STANDARD – ERA 1, STANDARD 2

Era 1, Standard 2: How early European exploration and colonization resulted in cultural and ecological interactions among previously unconnected peoples.

HISTORICAL THINKING STANDARDS 4 A, 4 B, & 4 C

Both Sides of the Coin
Number of People: 2   Time: 15 - 20 minutes   Grade Level 5

Materials: Quarters, the Internet
Description: Ask your child to tell you what is on each side of a quarter. There are reasons why George Washington is on one side. Discuss the historical reasons why he would be there. Why are the words, "Liberty" and "In God We Trust" on the same side? If you have an older coin, talk about the eagle and E Pluribus Unum. If you have a newer coin, you will find all kinds of history from each of the states pictured. If you or your child is not sure why something is on a coin from one state or another, find the answers on the Internet.

U.S. HISTORY STANDARD – ERA 2, STANDARD 3
Era 2, Standard 3: How the values and institutions of European economic life took root in the colonies, and how slavery reshaped European and African life in the Americas.
HISTORICAL THINKING STANDARD 4 C

Don't Tread on Me
Number of People: 2   Time: An hour   Grade Level 5

Materials: History books or the Internet, paper and pencil
Description: The American Revolution had a number of slogans created to express dissatisfaction with English rule and the colonist's desire to be an independent nation. "Don't Tread on Me" and "No Taxation without Representation" were two of those slogans. Ask your child to find other slogans of the American Revolution, discover what those slogans meant, and why they were important.

U.S. HISTORY STANDARD – ERA 3, STANDARDS 1, 2, & 3
Era 3, Standard 1: The causes of the American Revolution, the ideas and interests involved in forging the revolutionary movement, and the reasons for the American victory. Standard 2: The impact of the American Revolution of politics, economy, and society. Standard 3: The institutions and practices of government creased during the Revolution and how they were revised between 1787 and 1815 to create the foundation of the American political system based on the U.S. Constitution and the Bill of Rights.
HISTORICAL THINKING STANDARD 3 I

When did history "star"t in your scrapbook?

Historic Scrapbook
Number of People: 2 or more   Time: An hour

Grade Level **5**

Materials: Magazines, paper, glue, scissors

Description: Let your child make a historic scrapbook showing the development of the nation. These could be current events or events from a number of years ago. Let him look through your magazines for pictures of historic events and people or print pictures from the Internet. Have him mark the date of the event when he finds it. Let him arrange the pictures for the scrapbook from oldest events to the most recent. Have him write a description of each event and note the time of the event in the scrapbook.

U.S. HISTORY STANDARD - ERA 10, STANDARDS 1 AND 2

Era 10, Standard 1: Recent developments in foreign and domestic politics

Standard 2: Economic, social, and cultural developments in contemporary United States

HISTORICAL THINKING STANDARD 2 F

What we learned today...

_____

_____

_____

_____

_____

_____

Travelogue of the U.S. Capitals
Number of People: 2 or more   Time: 15 minutes   Grade Level **5**

Materials: A wait in the car

Description: While waiting in a drive-thru line for fast food, there is often nothing to do. In our family, in order to make better use of our time, I would pretend we were on a trip to different states in the country. Our job was to get from the capital of one state to the capital of another. I would say we are going to Arizona, and they would tell me we could visit their grandparents in its capital, Phoenix. Then I would decide to go to Colorado, and they needed to tell me that its capital, Denver, was the destination. Then I'd head for Utah. Someone would know the capital was Salt Lake City. Soon we would be getting our hamburgers, but if not, we would move on to the next state.

U.S. HISTORY STANDARD – ERA 10, STANDARD 2

Era 10, Standard 2: Economic, social, and cultural developments in contemporary United States.

HISTORICAL THINKING STANDARD 2 G

USA Search
Number of People: 2   Time: 30 minutes   Grade Level **5**

Materials: Map of the U.S.

Description: Name a state of the U.S. Let your child find that state on the map. Ask her to tell you the capital. If she doesn't know, she can study the map until she finds it. Keep working at it until she gets them all.

U.S. HISTORY STANDARD – ERA 10, STANDARD 2

Era 10, Standard 2: Economic, social, and cultural developments in contemporary United States.

HISTORICAL THINKING STANDARD 2 G

hat we learned today...

Create your own playbook activities!

History	Grade Level
Number of People: Time:	
Materials:	
Description:	

U.S. HISTORY LEARNING STANDARDS

HISTORICAL THINKING STANDARDS

History	Grade Level
Number of People: Time:	
Materials:	
Description:	

U.S. HISTORY LEARNING STANDARDS

HISTORICAL THINKING STANDARDS

Create your own playbook activities!

History　　　　　　　　　　　　　　　　　　　　　Grade Level
Number of People:　　Time:

Materials:

Description:

U.S. HISTORY LEARNING STANDARDS

HISTORICAL THINKING STANDARDS

History　　　　　　　　　　　　　　　　　　　　　Grade Level
Number of People:　　Time:

Materials:

Description:

U.S. HISTORY LEARNING STANDARDS

HISTORICAL THINKING STANDARDS

INDEX

ENGLISH LANGUAGE ARTS (ELA)	Page
ENGLISH LANGUAGE ARTS STANDARDs	4
Books for Kids	6
Comics Aloud	6
Library Days	7
Books and More Books	8
Read the Board	9
Bake a Cake	9
Read the Kitchen	10
Favorite Stories	10
Famous Read	11
Hang Man	12
Weekly Recipe	13
Kid Magazines	13
Movie Review	14
Notes	14
Vacation Diary	15
Cartoon Balloons	16
Directions	17
Pen Me	17
Writing More Email Letters	18
Wishes and Dreams	18
TV Talk	19
Project Practice	20
Play It	21
Ordering Out	21
Topical Questions	22
Crosswords	22
New Words from TV	23
What is the Theme?	24
It's a Myth	25
Books and Movies	25
Library Days Too	26
Magazines	26
Reading Around You	27
Listen to the Reading	28
TV Review	29
You Have Mail	29
Family Newspaper	30
Reports	30

Daily Journal	31
Ordering In	32
Your Video is Showing	33
Anecdotes are Personal Accounts	33
Weekly Readers Plus	34
Write-to-Me Grammar	34
Write-to-Me Spelling	35
Talk Time	36
Read Everything Again	37
Quotes	38
Library Days with a New Twist	38
Chapter Books	39
Movie Time	40
What Was That	41
Vacation Research	41
It's in the News	42
Scrabble	42
Listen to the Reading	43
Splain It	44
Penmanship Plus	45
Reporter Rewrite	45
Electronic Writing	46
Reports with Support	46
Writing Your Own Story	47
Take 20	48
PowerPoint	49
Crostics	49
Talking Down	50
Proverbial Sayings	50
What we learned today...	51
Create your own playbook activities	52-53
MATH	55
MATH LEARNING STANDARDs	57
Grocery Math	58
Breakfast Multiplication	59
How Much	59
Pizza Night	60
Family Math Night	60
License Math	61
License Numbers	62
Kitchen Measuring	63

Time to Tell	63
How Much for the Week?	64
We Need How Much?	64
Cookie Shapes	65
Mileage	66
Worth the Time	67
Catalog Days	67
Time Charts	68
Need a New Computer	68
Round About	69
Newspaper Shopping	70
Drying Your Hair Plus	71
Water Fractions	71
Trip Addition	72
Geometric Design	72
Parentheses Please	73
Algebra is Easy	74
Shopping Spree	75
Yahtzee	75
Recipe Add	76
Time to Go	76
What we learned today...	77
Create your own playbook activities	78-79
SCIENCE	81
SCIENCE LEARNING STANDARDS	82
Kitchen Sense	84
Mixtures and Solutions	85
Bubble Time	85
Cleaning Ashes from the Fireplace	86
Kitchen Matters	86
Guinea Pig Pets	87
Gold Lesson	88
Moonshine	89
Summer Light	89
Squeaky Hinge	90
Summer Wading	90
Rain Gauge	91
Science Cakes	92
Creating a Charge	93
Electric Hair	93
Salsa	94

Seed Study	94
Growing Fungi	95
Mineral Sales	96
Breaking Rocks	97
What we learned today...	98
Starch Detective	99
Cabbage Experiments	99
Oil and Water	100
Pinwheels	100
Weather or Not	101
Create your own playbook activities	102-103

HISTORY — 103

Learning Standards, History/Social Studies	106
Local Native American Folklore	116
School as Work	116
You are There	117
Local History	118
Bridging Gaps	119
Name that Park	119
Exploring Explorers	120
Exploring is Exploring	120
Picture This	121
Build a New Road	122
Dust Bowl Immigration	123
Know Your Representatives	123
Give Us Statehood	124
Your State's Historians	124
Water, Water Everywhere	125
Historic Letter	126
Tell the Truth	127
What State Am I?	127
Both Sides of the Coin	128
Don't Tread on Me	128
Travelogue of the U.S. Capitals	130
USA Search	130
What we learned today...	131
Create your own playbook activities	132-133

Parent Playbooks Activities Form

I have a favorite activity to include in an upcoming parent playbook. It's in the area of:

- [ ] English/Language Arts
- [ ] Math
- [ ] Science
- [ ] Social Studies

Grade Level: Preschool   K-2   3-5   6-8   9-12

Your Name: _____

Address: _____

City: _____ St: _____ Zip: _____

Email: _____

School child attends: _____

Location: _____

Mail to:
Engage! Press
2485 Notre Dame Blvd 370-170
Chico, CA 95928

Or by Fax or Email:
Fax: 530-899-8423
www.familyfriendlyschools.com

Create your own playbook activity

| Number of People: | Time: | Grade Level |

Materials:

Description:

Parent Playbooks Order Form

Grade	# of Copies	Per Copy	Total
Pre-Sch	_____	$19.95	_____
K-2	_____	$19.95	_____
3-5	_____	$19.95	_____
6-8	_____	$19.95	_____
Subtotal			_____
Tax			x _____
Total with tax			_____
Postage / Handling $3.00/bk			_____
Total			_____

Name: _____

Address: _____

City: _____ St: ____ Zip: _____

Phone: _____ Fax: _____

Email: _____

Check or money order #: _____

Purchase Order # _____

Mail to:
Engage! Press
2485 Notre Dame Blvd 370-170
Chico, CA 95928

Or by Fax or Email:
Fax: 530-899-8423
www.familyfriendlyschools.com

www.ingramcontent.com/pod-product-compliance
Lightning Source LLC
Chambersburg PA
CBHW080513110426
42742CB00017B/3100